Squier
ELECTRICS

TONY BACON

Squier
ELECTRICS

0 YEARS OF FENDER'S BUDGET GUITAR BRAND

SQUIER ELECTRICS
30 YEARS OF FENDER'S BUDGET GUITAR BRAND

TONY BACON

A BACKBEAT BOOK
First edition 2012
Published by Backbeat Books
An Imprint of Hal Leonard Corporation
7777 West Bluemound Road,
Milwaukee, WI 53213
www.backbeatbooks.com

Devised and produced for Backbeat Books by
Outline Press Ltd
2A Union Court, 20-22 Union Road,
London SW4 6JP, England
www.jawbonepress.com

ISBN: 978-1-61713-022-9

A catalogue record for this book is available from the British Library.

DESIGN: Paul Cooper Design
EDITOR: Siobhan Pascoe

Printed by Everbest Printing Co. Ltd, China

12 13 14 15 16 5 4 3 2 1

CONTENTS

SQUIER ELECTRICS

THE REFERENCE LISTING

" If you've ever played a classic Fender, you'll recognize the family resemblance immediately. **"**

PART OF PUBLICITY BLURB FOR FIRST SQUIER GUITARS SOLD IN THE USA, 1983

THE
SQUIER
ELECTRICS
STORY

SOMEWHERE IN AMERICA, at the end of 1978, Paul Stanley of Kiss sits down for an interview. Out of costume, bereft of his Kiss makeup and clothes and boots, he speeds through questions about his band's success – 20 million records sold, he guesses – and their recent Japanese tours. Talk turns to guitars. Stanley is a fan of the growing skills of the Japanese makers. "They obviously have the facilities to make anything," he says, recalling a trip to the headquarters of Ibanez, which makes his suitably flashy signature model. "That's a lot more than can be said for America at the moment. Japan really is the country of the future." [1]

This was a grim time for the American makers. The big two, Fender and Gibson, were suffering increasing costs, especially in manufacturing, and every few months the Japanese makers offered more serious competition. The Americans needed to find a way out of the mess if they were to survive. For Fender, the answer would come with a new brand, Squier, and with it the start of manufacturing instruments overseas. However, this strategy would take a while to develop, as we shall discover. For now, Fender's owner, CBS, considered the immediate problems.

Beginning in 1981, CBS took a radical step and recruited new blood to try to pump life into the ailing Fender operation by hiring key men from the American musical-instruments division of Yamaha, the big Japanese company famous for its pianos, electronics, and, increasingly, guitars. John McLaren was taken on as the new head of CBS Musical Instruments overall. Bill Schultz was the new president of the Fender/Rogers/Rhodes division (guitars/drums/keyboards), Dan Smith became director of marketing electric guitars, and Roger Balmer, who came from Music Man but had been at Yamaha before, was installed as head of marketing and sales. From within CBS, Bill Mendello, chief financial officer of the instruments division, relocated to California and based himself at Fender. These were the key managers who would guide the firm through the tricky years ahead.

Dan Smith, the new man in charge of guitars at Fender, says CBS brought in the team to turn around Fender's flagging reputation and to regain the market share the brand had lost since the late 70s. "At that point in time everybody hated what Fender had become," he recalls. "We thought we knew how bad it was, but we took it for granted that they could make Stratocasters and Telecasters the way they used to make them. We were wrong. So many things had been changed in the Fender factory at Fullerton."

Smith already knew that Fender quality was not good, and that everybody – players, dealers, the company itself – knew the quality was not good. Before Yamaha, he'd worked as a guitar repairer in Rochester, New York, and there Smith saw for himself some of the poor instruments his customers brought in. He worked at Yamaha from 1977, and when he visited dealers, they often wanted to talk more about how awful Fender and Gibson guitars were than about Yamaha.

When he arrived at Fender in 1981, Smith had an early shock as he toured the factory. "I remember looking at the body contours," he says. "People were complaining about contours, and here I am looking at racks of hundreds of guitars. Every one of those guitars had a different edge contour! We went and pulled guitars out of the warehouse, and we did a series of general re-inspections on 800-plus guitars. Out of those, I think only about 15 passed the existing criteria."[2]

One of his first plans was to revise the overall specifications of the Stratocaster, primarily by going back to a four-bolt neck-to-body joint. It was the method Fender had used from 1954 to 1971, at which point CBS introduced the three-bolt joint. The original was felt to be a more stable fixing. Smith says he also changed to "the right headstock", a reference to his revamped Strat's approximation of a pre-1965 head shape. The four-bolt Fender Standard Stratocaster started production at the company's Fullerton plant toward the end of 1981.

It was the latest in a long line of Fender models, and a further variation on one of their two main themes: the Stratocaster and the Telecaster. Leo Fender had started the company decades earlier, a development of his radio and repair store in Fullerton. He had a false start in 1945 with K&F, which he set up with musician Doc Kauffman to make lap-steel guitars and small amps, but in the following year he reorganised without Doc. At first he called the new firm Fender Manufacturing and then a year or two later the Fender Electric Instrument Company. Alongside Leo, Don Randall would become Fender's sales boss, Forrest White the factory manager, and Freddie Tavares would look after model development.

Fender continued to make lap-steels and amps, but in 1949 started work on the instrument we now know as the Fender Telecaster, the world's first commercial solidbody electric guitar. The guitar, named the Fender Esquire and then the Fender Broadcaster, went into production in 1950. It was renamed as the Fender Telecaster in 1951, the same year Fender introduced its revolutionary new electric solidbody Precision Bass.

Practicality and function ruled. They didn't care for the way established guitar-makers such as Gibson would hand-carve selected timbers. With the Telecaster, Fender turned the electric guitar into a factory product, stripped down to its essential elements, put together from easily assembled parts, and produced at a relatively affordable price. These methods made for easier, more consistent production – and a different sound. Not for Fender the woody Gibson-style jazz tone, but a clearer, spikier sound, something like a cross between a clean acoustic guitar and a cutting electric lap-steel.

Leo and Freddie Tavares listened hard to players' comments about the plain, workmanlike Tele, and they began to devise the guitar that became the Fender Stratocaster. It was launched in 1954, the first solidbody electric with three pickups. It also had a newly-designed built-in vibrato unit (or tremolo, as Fender called it) for pitch-bending effects, and the radically sleek solid body, based on the shape of the earlier Precision Bass, was contoured for the player's comfort. Even the jack mounting was new, recessed in a stylish plate on the body face. The Strat looked like no other guitar around – and owed more to contemporary car design than traditional guitar forms, especially in the flowing, sensual curves of that beautiful, timeless body. The Fender Strat would become the most popular, the most copied, the most desired, and very probably the most played solid electric guitar ever.

Fender introduced more models as the firm grew in confidence. In 1956, along came a pair of 'student' electrics, each with a shorter scale length than usual. Fender described the "three-quarter size" one-pickup Musicmaster and two-pickup Duo-Sonic as "ideal for students and adults with small hands", for players on a tight budget, and for those starting out on electric guitar and flocking to the music-store 'schools' that were springing up everywhere across the USA. These were cheaper guitars, aimed at beginners, and as such you could say they foreshadowed the idea behind the Squier brand. Fender later added further student models: the Mustang, in 1964, effectively a Duo-Sonic with a vibrato, and the Bronco, in 1967, a single-pickup model with simple vibrato.

New for 1958, the Fender Jazzmaster was more expensive than the Strat. Immediately striking was its unusual offset-waist body and, for the first time on a Fender, a separate rosewood fingerboard glued to the customary maple neck. The vibrato system was new, too, with an ill-conceived 'lock-off' facility intended to prevent tuning problems if a string should break. The model marked a distinct change for Fender, a real effort to extend the scope and appeal of its guitar line. But the Jazzmaster was never as popular as the Strat or Tele.

The next new design from Fender was the Jaguar, which showed up in 1962. It had the offset-waist body shape of the Jazzmaster and shared that guitar's separate bridge and vibrato unit, but most players ignored its spring-loaded string mute at the bridge. It was the first Fender with 22 frets (the others had 21), and it had a slightly shorter scale-length than usual for Fenders (closer to Gibson's standard, providing a different feel). Like the Jazzmaster, the Jaguar has never enjoyed the sustained success of the Strat and Tele.

No one outside the company expected the news in January 1965, when the mighty Columbia Broadcasting System Inc, better known as CBS, announced it had bought the Fender companies. A music-trade magazine reported in somewhat shocked tones: "The purchase price of $13 million is by far the highest ever offered in the history of the [musical instrument] industry for any single manufacturer, and was about two million dollars more than CBS paid recently for the New York Yankees baseball team."[3] In the years that followed, the sale to CBS would provoke frustration and even anger among guitar players and collectors, some of whom considered so-called 'pre-CBS' instruments – in other words those made prior to the beginning of 1965 – as superior to Fenders made in the 70s. And while this has come to be seen as a rather simplistic generalisation, CBS certainly did make changes. According to insiders, the problem with CBS was it believed that all it needed to do was pour a great deal of money into Fender. Certainly Fender's sales increased and profits rose. But quality did suffer. And there was a significant clash of cultures. The new CBS men, often trained engineers with college degrees, believed in high-volume production. Fender's old guard were long-serving craft workers without formal qualifications.

CBS retained Leo's services as a special consultant in research and development. He was set to work away from the Fender buildings and allowed to tinker just as much as he liked – with very little effect on the Fender product lines. He completed a few projects for CBS but left when his five-year contract expired in 1970. He went on to design and make instruments for Music Man and G&L, and he died in 1991. Most of the rest of the old guard gradually departed from the new CBS-owned Fender. Forrest White went in 1967, going on to work with Leo at Music Man, and at CMI, which owned Gibson, and Rickenbacker. He died in 1994. Don Randall resigned from CBS in 1969, and formed Randall Electric Instruments, which he sold in 1987. He died in 2008.

New models continued to appear in the CBS period. The Electric XII had been on the drawing board before the sale, and it hit the stores later in 1965. The Beatles and The Byrds had just made electric 12-strings popular, and they both used Rickenbackers. Fender joined the battle with its rather belated XII, although an innovation was the guitar's 12-saddle bridge, which allowed precise adjustments of individual string height and intonation. Fender also tried a new line of hollowbody electrics, aimed to compete with Gibson and Gretsch, but like the XII, the Coronado, Montego, and LTD models were shortlived.

Toward the end of the 60s came firm evidence of CBS wringing every last drop of potential income from unused factory stock that would otherwise have been written off. Two shortlived guitars – the Maverick (whch was also known as the Custom), and the Swinger – soaked up bits and pieces from leftover Electric XIIs, Musicmasters, Bass Vs, and Mustangs.

Fender introduced a few variations on the Tele. The Thinline, with a weight-reduced body that bore a single f-hole, came along in 1968, while the Custom of 1972 replaced the Tele's regular neck pickup with a humbucker, the first to appear on a Fender. Similar dabbling led to the two-humbucker Strat-necked Tele Deluxe of 1973. In 1976, the company made another attempt at thinline hollowbody electrics with the shortlived Starcaster, which again tried to compete (unsuccessfully) with Gibson's ever-popular ES line. By this time, Fender had a five-acre facility under one roof in Fullerton and employed over 750 workers, who churned out mostly Strats and Teles. There was hardly a major guitarist who hadn't played a Fender at some time. At the start of the decade, that was mostly thanks to the continuing influence of Jimi Hendrix. Leading Fender players of the time included Eric Clapton, who first adopted a Strat around 1970, Ritchie Blackmore, who took his Strat to even louder amplified extremes, and James Burton, whose paisley Tele graced many a country-flavoured session. Toward the end of the 70s, as punk and synthesizers seemed set to devalue and even eclipse electric guitars in pop music, Mark Knopfler's clean melodic tones in Dire Straits underlined the apparently timeless appeal of the Stratocaster.

In 1981, Bill Schultz, Fender's new president, told a NAMM trade-association magazine, *Up Beat*, about the changes that were under way "to create a virtually new Fender/Rogers/Rhodes". He knew the industry was most concerned about the poor quality of instruments coming from the Fullerton factory in recent years – so he said what Fender's dealers wanted to hear. "There'll be an increased emphasis on quality control at every level of the organization," Schultz said, "from the director of operations to the workers on the production line."[4] In fact, part of the large investment package Schultz recommended was aimed at modernising the factory. This more or less immediately stopped production while new machinery was brought in and staff were re-trained.

Bill Mendello, then the chief financial officer of CBS's instruments division and a new resident at Fender, is in no doubt today when he recalls the main problem they faced. "The factory at Fullerton was totally inadequate," he says with a groan. "So we shut down the facility and redid the whole thing. We also went out and cancelled a lot of dealers and added new ones. We realised the guitar line was stale. We did all those things right away. But while we tried to fix Fender as it was, we realised that the world had changed. The Japanese had changed the rules."[5]

When Japanese guitar-makers copied classic American instrument designs in the early 70s, most Western makers didn't see much to worry about. Gradually, the Japanese improved the quality of their guitars, but some American companies had their heads stuck firmly in the sand. Dave Gupton, vice president of Fender in 1978, said: "Fender is not adversely affected by the Japanese copies as perhaps some of the other major manufacturers, because we have been able to keep our costs pretty much in line."[6] That casual attitude changed dramatically in a few short years. By the start of the 80s, the high quality of many Japanese guitars meant that instruments built there were making a real impact on the international guitar market. Many were copies of Fender and Gibson models, and especially the Strat, which was enjoying renewed popularity.

Ibanez was one of the earliest Japanese brands to make a noise in the USA and Europe. The brand's electric guitars first arrived in the States in 1972, through distributor Elger, and reached the UK around the same time, through Summerfield. The Ibanez line, made at the Fujigen factory in Japan, consisted of barefaced copies of mostly

Fender and Gibson designs. Ibanez exploited a new demand among a number of guitarists who were looking for old 'vintage' guitars from the 50s and 60s because they disliked the poor quality of some new instruments. An Ibanez ad from 1973 boasted: "We don't have to tell you about the demand for oldies. Ibanez 'new oldies' are made to look like, play like, and sound like the models that inspired them. And just to show you that our nostalgia is in the right place, most Ibanez 'new oldies' sell for less than the 'old oldies' did when they were first introduced."[7]

The early copies weren't very good. But legal action by US makers – as well as a general inclination by the Japanese to improve their business – led to better quality as the 70s progressed. "Players could relate to this Japanese product," Mendello says. "I could relate to it, too. In 1970, I would not have bought a Japanese car if you'd paid me. In 1980, I owned a couple of Japanese cars. They had become good manufacturers."[8]

Ibanez typified the abilities and intentions of the best Japanese makers. The company continued to copy for a while but seemed more interested in original designs, and in 1976 it launched the refined Artist double-cutaway solidbody and the angular Iceman. It was the start of a new phase in Japanese electric guitars, where quality and design matched and in some cases – given the problems in the USA – exceeded that of American instruments.

These developments weren't confined to Ibanez. The new team at Fender had come from Yamaha and were well aware of the advances made there. Kanda Shokai's house brand, Greco, was another mark of quality copies, and like Ibanez they were made by Fujigen. In 1981, Greco's Stratocaster copy line ranged from the SE-380, which retailed at 38,000 yen, up to the SE-1200, at 120,000 yen. A straightforward conversion into US dollars at the time gave an equivalent range of about $260 to $530. That same year, Fender's cheapest Stratocaster retailed for $720.

But there was one Japanese name in particular that exercised the team at Fender. That was Tokai. As far as many guitarists were concerned, Tokai was doing a grand job. The firm began soon after the end of World War II in Hamamatsu as a general instrument factory. It offered contract manufacturing to other Japanese companies but also developed its own brand, launching Tokai electric guitars in 1967. Ten years later, the copies began.

Tokai's Strat copies were called the Springy Sound models. The smiles that the name brought became wider when players plugged in these guitars. They blatantly copied the look and build and playability of classic-period Stratocasters. The overall vibe was close to the original, but the details were hard to ignore, too. For example, the font that Tokai used for the logo on the vintage-shape headstock was designed to look just like an old-style Fender 'spaghetti' logo, and the tiny line underneath where a genuine vintage Strat said "With Synchronized Tremolo" instead had the mischievous message: "This Is An Exact Replica Of The Good Old Strat." That hyperbole wasn't far from the truth: it was a well made, easy-playing, vintage-like Stratocaster with good pickups (some had DiMarzios) and an obsessive attention to detail. Richard Thompson – who played an original 50s Strat and adored American guitars – checked out one of these Tokai Springy Sound models. He said: "It looks like the Japanese have finally cracked it."[9]

You can imagine the reaction at Fender. Dan Smith: "Regardless of how bad the originators might be at making a product, that doesn't give anybody else licence to copy it. Tokai would use this line that they're just carrying on the real tradition … and all that rubbish. That used to irritate me no end. To copy us wholesale, down to the last screw, *still* irritates me." Another excuse that Fender would hear is that it is culturally acceptable in the East to copy, and that the practice is not frowned upon there like it is in the West. "I went to Japan over 50 times, and probably another 30 times to Korea," Smith says, "and I never totally understood that concept. But these companies certainly didn't feel like they were doing anything wrong."[10]

Fender tried legal action. It authorised US Customs to confiscate imports of guitars that used Fender's headstock shapes and, dramatically, to cut off the heads of offending instruments. *Billboard* reported one such action: "Following an earlier warning issued by the Fender/Rogers/Rhodes division of CBS Musical Instruments, US Customs agents recently seized two shipments of guitars illegally using the familiar Fender headstocks and shipped to San Francisco from Japan."[11] Fender's distributor in the UK and Germany threatened Tokai's trade outlets in those countries with similar moves. "But it was such an overwhelming situation that we couldn't fight it only with legal means," recalls Roger Balmer, Fender's new head of marketing and sales. "We had to take other steps."

Balmer says the problems of foreign competition that faced the new team at Fender were embodied in one overwhelming sales statistic. He remembers an early and difficult presentation that he made to the CBS top brass. "I told them that Fender had about 15 percent of the worldwide Fender-type market, and that this was declining. The other 85 percent was a variety of Fender copies and Fender-like products. The strategy Fender adopted to deal with this before we came along was, basically, a legal strategy, run by their lawyers. But it just wasn't getting the job done. The results were not coming. We were losing. I said that no sports team or company can hope to succeed playing only defence in its home market and that we had to go on to the offence at home and internationally."[12]

"We had to stop this plethora of copies," Smith agrees. "These companies were ripping us off. What we really needed to do was to get the Japanese where it hurt – back in their own marketplace."[13] The new Fender execs were aware that Japanese makers made their biggest profits at home, where they sold at relatively high prices, compared to the cheaper prices they charged in the USA and Europe in order to increase their competitive edge and market share. "We knew that if we could find a way to sell Japanese-manufactured Fender-branded products in the Japanese market at prices below companies like Tokai and the other copycats," Smith says, "we would eat into their business at home, forcing them to raise their prices abroad to remain profitable – because they were going to have to lower their prices at home to be competitive. Our ultimate goal was to force them to stop copying us and to develop their own unique products."[14]

The new management team decided that one way to revive Fender was to copy itself. The plan was to re-create the guitars that many Japanese makers were diligently copying and that many players and collectors were spending large sums of money to acquire. These were the so-called vintage guitars made during Fender's golden years in the 50s and 60s.

Freddie Tavares, one of the original Fender men from the 50s, still worked in Fender R&D in 1980, when he began work on a Vintage Telecaster. The idea was to re-create a 1952-style original, prompted by an idea from marketing manager Paul Bugelski. It was planned to be the first modern reissue of a vintage-style Fender guitar. At the July NAMM music-trade show in 1981, organised by the National Association of Music Merchants, Fender showed a prototype. Dan Smith arrived at the company a month later and was not pleased with what he saw. "This supposed '52 Telecaster had a polyester finish, the wrong body shape – a whole bunch of stuff wrong with it. I told them we can't ship that. So we shut down the Vintage reissue series. We brought in Ted Greene, a great guitar player here in Southern California, who had 14 old Broadcasters and Nocasters and Telecasters. We spent a lot of time with him and his Teles, making sure we had all the details right."[15]

The new Fender team needed still more tangible information to assist in their proposed re-creations of vintage models. R&D man John Page travelled with Smith to a vintage-guitar dealer in Illinois, Ax In Hand, where they took further measurements and photographs and paint-tests from the relevant old guitars – and they also made some purchases. "We left having bought perfect examples of each era," Smith says. "We spent $5,600 on a '57 Precision, '60 Jazz Bass, and a '61 Strat – which for Fender at the time was ludicrous. We went out and bought back our own product!"[16] Now Smith and his colleagues had all the data they needed to go ahead with a new series of Vintage reissue Fender guitars and basses.

Meanwhile, Smith, Schultz, and Balmer discussed the plan to start parallel production of Fender guitars in Japan. Yamano Music had been Fender's distributor there for nearly 20 years, since 1963, but as they did not sell beyond their own chain of stores – they had "sales offices" in Tokyo, Osaka, Nagoya, and Fukuoka – Fender wanted an additional distributor with a broader reach. Schultz and Balmer talked to a number of potential candidates and decided upon Kanda Shokai. Balmer already had a good relationship with Kanda, who distributed Music Man products in Japan – Balmer had worked at Music Man before he came to Fender. Kanda had the wider scope Fender wanted and a reputation for tenacious and successful selling. A bonus was that Kanda had close links with the leading manufacturer Fujigen, which produced Kanda's house brand,

Greco, as well as Ibanez and other quality instruments. "We went to Japan and toured a number of factories, Tokai and others," Balmer recalls. "Actually, we had ideas of taking one of them over or buying one of them out, but I saw that as a false concept. Fujigen looked like a good choice."[17] Smith says: "I know the meeting with Tokai went badly. They basically told Bill Schultz that they didn't need to work with Fender and, in fact, that Tokai would bury us in a couple of years. Big mistake."[18]

The joint venture, which was given the name Fender Japan, was announced at a press conference at the Hotel Grand Palace in Tokyo on March 11 1982. It combined the forces of the Fender/Rogers/Rhodes division of CBS Musical Instruments, the Kanda Shokai Corporation, and Yamano Music. The principals present at the launch were Schultz, Balmer, and Smith from Fender; Chitoshi Kojima, president of Kanda; and Masamitsu Yamano, president of Yamano.

Journalists at the gathering heard that the new company was ready to start in May and would offer budget versions of Stratocasters, Telecasters, and basses at various quality levels, at first in quantities of around 3,000 to 3,500 guitars and basses per month. Fender USA licensed Fender Japan the right to build Fender instruments within Japan and to sell them on the Japanese market. Kanda and Yamano would both sell them in Japan, and Yamano would also continue to sell imported US-made Fenders. Yamano's boss Masamitsu Yamano insisted that the Japanese and American lines would not compete with each other. "We hope that beginners will become accustomed to moderately-priced Fenders," he said, "and that eventually they will step up their instruments to the American higher-ticket models."[19]

Fender moved forward with its newly-planned Vintage reissues, having announced them in February at the Winter 1982 NAMM trade show in Anaheim, California. "CBS have finally seemed to realise that players actually like Fenders the way Leo used to make them, so they have copied their competitors and copied themselves," wrote British guitar-maker Peter Cook in a report on the show.[20] The series consisted of a maple-neck '57-style Stratocaster, a rosewood-fingerboard '62 Stratocaster, a '52 Telecaster, and a couple of basses. Production was planned to start at the troubled Fullerton factory in California. At about the same time, Fujigen, the manufacturer chosen by the joint venture, started production of the equivalent Japanese-made series for Fender Japan at its facility in Matsumoto.

Fender Japan's first instruments, the Vintage series, were announced on May 7 to a further press conference at Tokyo's Hotel Grand Palace. The Fujigen-made line consisted of the five models – '57 and '62 Strats, '52 Tele, two basses – each in line with the Japanese system that offered two or three different price-points for each model, in this case dependent upon the quality of construction and finish and whether US parts, including pickups, were used. Retail prices ranged from ¥65,000 to ¥115,000, about $260 to $460 at the time. "The establishment of Fender Japan," Masamitsu Yamano told the assembled press, "will sweep away the Fender copies sold here in Japan as well as in other markets."[21]

Fujigen was in a strong position to manufacture the new Fender Japan guitars, because for some time it had made the excellent Greco-brand copies for Kanda. "The best-selling part of the Greco line in Japan was their copy models," Smith says. "They made extremely accurate copies of Fender, Gibson, Gretsch, and Rickenbacker guitars and basses. This made it pretty easy for us to start up with a product line that was already in production – which was probably the only benefit to us from the copy situation." He says that Kanda paid a heavy price for their involvement in Fender Japan when it lost distribution rights for some of its top Japanese brands, including Ibanez and probably Roland. "I believe Kanda's situation was viewed in Japan as a slap in the face to Japanese manufacturers," Smith says. "There was an awful lot of nationalistic pride involved."

Smith spent plenty of time at the Fujigen factory to develop the new Fender Japan instruments. He determined the models and their prices and worked with the people who would produce the guitars. "I spent a couple of days just carving necks to the shapes and specifications we wanted," he recalls. "Since we were in the middle of setting up the US-made vintage reissue series, I had the data from that research to draw from, although a lot of the stuff they were making already was very accurate. Fujigen had a lot of it pretty much nailed because of the almost religious attention to detail of the Japanese consumer. But I brought pictures with me and I brought measurements and specifications from the vintage guitars we'd bought and from others that we'd examined."[22]

Nick Sugimoto had run the R&D department at Fujigen since 1978, following a period when he worked in the States for Elger, Ibanez's American partner. He remembers well the many enjoyable meetings with Smith and how he worked through the samples of pickups, hardware, pickguards, even a catalogue or two. "He sent me out a magazine," Sugimoto says, "and he said I want to make this, and this, and this. So where are the original drawings, I asked him? We don't have any drawings, he said. OK, well, Fujigen were building the Greco copies of Fender. So I made calculations by mixing the data from Fujigen's drawings of Greco guitars and the photographs in the magazine."

Sugimoto says that when Fujigen made Greco copies, in each case they first acquired a real vintage original to work from. "We bought the actual guitars, broke them down, measured the whole thing," he explains. "We discovered exactly how they would make something like that, in order to precisely make the Greco instruments. So when we came to make the Fender Japan guitars, we knew what we were doing. We could be critically accurate, with the dimensions just right, exactly as our own drawings. The US-made Fenders at that time were not so accurate."[23] Fender knew this, too. "At the time," Smith says, "the US product was of questionable quality, and the Japanese-made product was of unquestionably better quality."[24] The Fujigen factory was located in Matsumoto, Nagano Prefecture, about 120 miles west of Tokyo. Fuji Gen Gakki Seizou Kabushikigaisha –

which translates as the Fuji Stringed-Instrument Manufacturing Corporation – produced its first guitar, a basic nylon-string acoustic, in 1960, and within a couple of years had added electrics.

Fujigen's factory was in a beautiful area, sometimes called the Japanese alps, with snow and skiing in the winter. It's a hit with sightseers. It's also an area known for people with woodworking expertise, and there were a number of furniture makers and many guitar-makers around – Matsumoku (Aria) and Moridaira (Morris), for example.

In an early-80s interview, the boss at Fujigen, Yuuichirou Yokouchi, explained that he became a dairy farmer after World War II but set up Fujigen after meeting Yutaka Mimura, a businessman. They started the firm in a converted cowshed. Fujigen enjoyed great success in the 60s, exporting to the USA and building a proper factory in 1965, but Yokouchi said there was a downturn the following year when the USA doubled customs duties on imported electrics. This prompted a focus on the domestic market.

By 1969, business was still poor, and as a result Mimura departed. Yokouchi was in charge. He steered Fujigen to new success through the 70s, and by the time Fender knocked on his door the company was in good shape. During the 80s interview, Yokouchi showed the journalist Fujigen's four CNC (computer-controlled) routers and explained that he was impressed by the way US makers used them to ensure the guitars they manufactured were consistent. "Producing the same result is such a key point in our mechanisation," Yokouchi said. "Of course, many processes are still done manually, by hand, and that is important. If the entire process could be done by machines, the companies with bigger capital could easily steal our business. Manual skills are so important, which is why we encourage our people to master the skills – and we protect our people, because they are the company's biggest asset."[25]

Fujigen outsourced a number of jobs to small firms, known in Japan as gaichuus, for painting, sanding, and so on. In that 80s interview with Yokouchi, the journalist saw many small sheds on the Fujigen site where self-employed ex-workers would do this work. "They did not just fire employees or cut down numbers by automating the processes," he wrote. "Instead they gave the employees the choice to stay, by allowing them to use the space within the site for free and supplying them raw materials. As a result, they created something like their own sub-contract factories, like subsidiaries sticking close to the parent company."[26] Fujigen also had a working relationship with another guitar factory, Dyna Gakki, which later would make some of the Fender Japan guitars, including Squiers.

Smith recalls that when he first visited, Fujigen had around 100 employees spread among eight or so buildings, and it wasn't the most modern guitar factory he'd seen. "Yamaha, for example, had a lot of high-end equipment and specially designed machines, pretty hi-tech for the time," Smith says. "Fujigen was more like Fender. There was a lot of stuff that was pretty much old-school. They did have some new equipment, but nothing like they and Fender would incorporate later, and, at the time, nothing like the kind of equipment at Yamaha. But there was plenty of pride in what they did, and the factory was very clean. The machinery was all up to snuff and all the fixtures were well maintained. It was a really good traditional 50s and 60s-style guitar manufacturing facility."[27]

Smith found the Fujigen factory something of a relief compared to the difficulties he faced back at Fender's American plant in Fullerton. "After maybe eight months of dealing with Fender," he says, "it was a real pleasure going to the Fujigen factory. The people there were as good as any I've ever known. Just great people. And they became one of the largest manufacturers in their country over probably the next ten years or so, which meant they steadily modernised the plant."[28]

Yokouchi was, of course, aware that the new relationship with Fender was a great boost for his company. He said: "In addition to the Greco and Ibanez guitars we make, which are Japan's top guitar brands, to also welcome Fender, one of the most successful guitar brands in America, is a huge honour for a manufacturer like us." Producing instruments for these three brands helped Fujigen keep down costs, he explained. "I am aware that sometimes guitars made by the same factory end up competing with each other in the market, but I think this is outweighed by the benefit of keeping costs low by producing 10,000 guitars a month, which we do now."[29]

As you might expect, Fender's move to Japanese production was not entirely popular back home. Some Americans still resented Japan as a matter of course, because of things that had happened in World War II. At the Fullerton plant in California, many workers, already beset by changes, did not react well to the news. "It became increasingly difficult to produce at Fullerton," Roger Balmer says. "We wanted to, but, more and more, it just wasn't economically feasible. The skills that were required were disappearing. And that reinforced the idea of Fender Japan. We needed to make changes." What form did Fullerton's objections to Japanese production take? "You can imagine. We had unions. Within Fender itself, and where I worked in Fullerton, it became very difficult. And understandably so, in a way, because it concerned jobs. There was fear. But we had to do something. Fender's survival was at stake, and these changes were absolutely necessary and the right thing to do."[30]

The changes under way at the Fullerton factory, which had effectively closed the plant, meant that the US-made versions of the new Vintage series would not appear until early 1983, and Fullerton did not really regain full speed until around the start of 1984. No such holdups detained Fender Japan, who worked fast to bring their Fender Vintage series to market. The new models were in the Japanese shops around May 1982. Smith and his colleagues at Fullerton HQ received samples of the Japanese guitars well before American production started. He remembers their reaction to the quality of this new line of Fender re-creations. "Everybody came up to inspect them," Smith says, "and the guys almost cried, because the Japanese product was so good. It was what we were having a hell of a time trying to do."[31]

The legendary Tele player Steve Cropper saw an early sample of a '52 Telecaster and praised the instrument. He guessed at the kind of thinking going on at Fender as they tried to reproduce the originals. "'Look, we're having more and more complaints about our newer guitars; it's time to get back in touch with the musicians.' I think [Fender] were making a real effort to go out and find out what people really thought," Cropper said.[32]

At the same time as the move to a separate Fender Japan operation, Fender considered the need for models to sell elsewhere at competitive prices. Many imported guitars in the USA and Europe were pretty good and relatively cheap. Fullerton's instruments, aside from the quality complaints, were proving expensive and could not provide what was needed. In fact, Fender had already attempted to deal with the problem, without success.

The Fender Lead models, introduced in 1979, were intended as simple US-made budget double-cutaway solids. But the Leads ended up retailing for $399: hardly the cheap solution Fender wanted. They were gone from the line within a few years. The original Fender Bullet involved a more complicated story and Fender's first, uncomfortable experience of offshore manufacturing – the term used by Americans for anything made outside the United States.

John Page, who would go on to run Fender's Custom Shop from the mid 80s, started work at Fender in 1978. He spent a few months on the production line before he moved to R&D. His first full guitar project as a designer was a fresh stab at a budget-price solid: the single-cutaway Bullet. "The marketing directive to me was to produce a guitar that the factory could make for $65," Page recalls. He had to consider money-saving from the outset. He devised a combined steel pickguard and bridge, he found surplus Mustang pickups in the factory, and he opted wherever possible for cheap but effective materials.

At first, the plan was to produce the Fender Bullet at Fullerton, Page says. Then management decided they wanted to make the neck and body even cheaper, and the suggestion was they contract the guitar to Samick, a Korean firm. "Someone from the finance department, who knew nothing about guitars, went over there," Page says. "He met with them to work out the import paperwork and sign a purchasing agreement – and as an added 'bonus' he agreed to a loosening of the setup specs in exchange for them lowering the cost by $1.50. So he came back and said OK, we're going to make them out of Philippine mahogany plywood – and, oh, they said they can make them cheaper if the strings are higher off the neck." Page's reply is unprintable.

Page remembers the call when the first shipment of Fender Bullets from Korea showed up in California in 1981. "I have an image of walking down there and seeing racks with hundreds of my first design in them. That was a personal rush! But other than that, what I remember is a lot of trouble with them."[33] Fender decided not to have the Bullets made entirely in Korea, and so at first the instruments were assembled in the States using Korean-manufactured parts. Even this did not produce guitars of a high enough standard, and by late 1981 the Bullets shifted to full American production. Fender's first experience of overseas manufacturing was over. The Bullets lasted until 1983, when various shortlived double-cutaway versions were also produced. The Bullet name was briefly shelved – but, as we'll discover, it would be reactivated at various times for a number of low-cost Squier models.

The problem remained: how to make a budget Fender of good quality that could sell at a competitive price among the East Asian imports? Several of Fender's distributors pressed for such an instrument, even though there was an inherent danger. If a cheaper line proved too successful, it might damage a distributor's still-profitable sales of US-made Fenders. And while the quality of those was an issue, it certainly hadn't killed sales. "It's kind of hard to believe," Smith says, "but one of the best years sales-wise in Fender's history, prior to our new team coming there, was in 1979 … when they made some of the biggest crap that they ever produced."[34]

Martin Fredman was sales and marketing director at one of Fender's most important distributors, CBS/Fender. The company, based in England, was started in 1973 by Ivor Arbiter and sold Fender products to dealers in the UK and Germany as well as the Netherlands, Belgium, and Luxembourg. "I recommended to Fender that they ought to be making a cheaper range, because there were so many others trying to copy the shape and so on," Fredman recalls. "Tokai were the main instigators – they were copying the Fender range as a whole and selling it cheaper. I said to Bill Schultz: Fender themselves ought to be doing this."[35] Fredman was not alone: other distributors said the same thing to Fender HQ. It was time to act.

A solution was staring Fender in the face. The Fullerton factory in California had its problems and, among other things, was incapable of producing a cheap, decent guitar. But what about the new Fender Vintage line about to roll off the Fujigen line in Japan? The deal with the Japanese, and indeed Fender USA's intention, was that these guitars would initially be for sale only in Japan. What if they could somehow be sold elsewhere? "We had started the product line in Japan," Dan Smith says, "and we felt that it would be perfect competition for what our European dealers were facing with the influx of copy models." [36]

An idea quickly developed to produce some even less expensive models in the Fender Japan line and add an identifying logo, and to market these as a separate line, at first only in Europe. The simple addition to the headstock was a new "Squier Series" logo on the tip – an area blank anyway on Telecasters, and where vintage-style Stratocasters usually had an "Original Contour Body" logo. A large "Fender" logo, a model-name logo, and a "Made In Japan" logo would all remain as on the other Fender Japan models. But how

■ Around the early 80s, Fender faced competition from Japanese makers, such as Tokai (ad, *right*), who copied its classic designs. Another was Greco, whose **copies** (main guitar) were produced in Japan by **Fujigen** (workshops *above and left*). Fujigen (entrance sign, *opposite*) also made Ibanez guitars – and would soon be making Fenders and Squiers. Fender tried to make **budget models** in the USA to compete, such as the Bullet (*right*) and Lead (ad, *far right*), but without success.

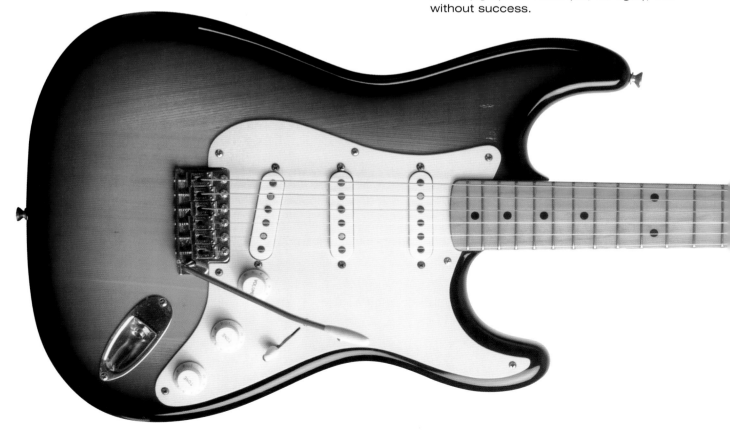

SQUIER ELECTRICS

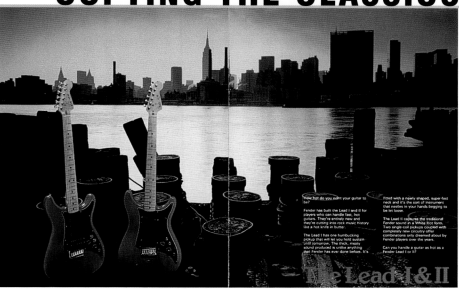

1982 Fender Bullet Red

1981 Greco Spacey Sound SE-500 Sunburst

did that rather unusual name "Squier" end up on the headstock? Fender needed a suitable name in a hurry. There was no time to select and register a new name, so it was a matter of looking through the existing musical brandnames that CBS owned. Smith recalls that Roger Balmer did the searching and hit on the old Squier strings brandname sitting in the CBS portfolio. "He'd been through all the product line names that we had, and that was his idea," Smith says.[37] Balmer's memory is foggier. "Well, I don't remember that so clearly," he laughs, trying his best to recall events from 30 years ago. "The list of registered names that CBS owned and which also had a long pedigree were very limited. So it was pretty obvious that we would lean toward Squier."[38]

V.C. Squier was a string-making firm that CBS had acquired as part of the package when it bought Fender and its associated companies in 1965. Even then, Squier was an old name in the music trade. Victor Carroll Squier, a violin-maker based in Michigan, started to make strings as a sideline around 1895. The strings did well, and soon they became the most important part of the firm's business.

Victor Carroll Squier was born in Battle Creek, Michigan, in 1866. His father, Jerome Bonaparte Squier, a travelling shoe-maker and later a violin-maker, was often away from home. Jerome was divorced from Victor's mother, Olive Brown Squier, in 1873, and for a couple of years he took Victor and Victor's sister Effie around on his travels, at first to Ohio, then New York, then New Jersey. The children moved back in with their mother, in Battle Creek, when Victor was eight years old.

In 1883, he went to Boston. His father had finally settled down there, and Squier senior invited 16-year-old Victor to come and work at his violin workshop. "This appealed to me greatly as I was naturally inclined to woodwork," Victor Squier recalled later. "I applied myself with great interest and enthusiasm." He stayed for about seven years, on and off, and learned from his father and a few other makers. He found out as much as he could about the techniques of violin building and made the most of Boston's lively music scene. "I became an expert craftsman," he said. "I made many violins and repaired great numbers, and I met the great players of bow instruments who visited the workshops."[39]

Squier set up on his own in 1890, establishing a violin-making shop back home in Battle Creek. His daughter, Carlotta, remembered: "Many times, in early years, he had to be pulled away from his bench to come to meals and rest."[40] Squier made good violins, some of which he sold to customers in Chicago and elsewhere. He found a ready market among amateur makers for kits of parts, which prompted a successful mail-order business. At one point, Squier had six violin-makers working in the shop, and when he died in 1949, at the age of 82, his firm's total production was estimated at 950 violins, violas, and cellos.

He had started to make strings around 1895, at first as an experiment, but soon they sold well and contributed a great deal to the firm's livelihood. The string-making, Squier remembered, "finally ran away from other activities, and in 1918 the business was incorporated, and a large modern brick and stone two-story-and-basement block was erected".[41] The violin-making was shunted off to a smaller shop in Battle Creek, and Squier hired his half-brother, Raymond Gould, to manage the string business. James 'Gus' Crawford, Squier's childhood friend who had joined the firm in 1892, concocted some string-winders from a few old sewing machines. This boosted production to 1,000 uniform-quality strings a day from each machine.

Squier's grand-daughter, Carol Sievert, remembered her grandfather's story about one particular visit to a music store. Squier told her: "I called on Charles Grinnell in Detroit in the early days, only to hear Mr Grinnell laugh at my string business. Mr Grinnell bought strings abroad. When he received a sample shipment of Squier products, however, he acknowledged his error, and from then on has carried Squier strings ever since."[42]

Squier was a keen theatregoer and an amateur actor and playwright. He wrote about the violin, too, and in 1944 produced a small book, *Antonio Stradivari: His Life And Work 1644–1737*, about his hero, the greatest Italian violin-maker. It shows Squier's heart was in violins, not strings. He relates the facts of Stradivari's life and then writes a fictionalised account, and in one part has Stradivari ruminating on his famous varnish. All violin-makers, including Squier, sought to analyse and understand this substance, believing it to be the secret ingredient of the Strad sound. Squier dedicated the book to his father, for "example, training, and council".

The Squier company added a further building to the string factory in 1927. During World War II, the strings sold particularly well, especially overseas, because the war had smashed the capabilities of the established string-makers in Germany and Japan. Squier reported at the time that he exported to Mexico, Cuba, New Zealand, Australia, China, Thailand, and Indonesia. Squier's daughter, Carlotta, later recalled that he learned to speak German to help his dealings with German violin firms, from whom he ordered inexpensive violins and parts. She said Squier also bought from firms in Czechoslovakia and Japan. "This merchandise sold for less money and served the beginning student," she explained.[43] The same argument would apply 40 years later when the Squier brand appeared on Japanese-made guitars.

Squier's Electro-Amp strings were among the first devised especially for the experimental electric guitars that appeared in the 30s, and later the firm headed the move to gauged sets of strings. Leo Fender's company began to use Squier strings in the early 50s and came to rely on Squier as a supplier. After Victor's death in 1949, his half-brother, Raymond Gould, continued to run the string-making division. Gould died in 1961, and soon V.C. Squier was sold to Fender, which used the Squier factory in Battle Creek as its main string-making facility. Fender's parent company CBS acquired V.C. Squier along with Fender in 1965 (although two Squier employees had split from the

SQUIER ELECTRICS

VICTOR'S STRINGS

1982 Fender Squier Series Stratocaster '62 Sunburst

■ **Victor Carroll Squier** opened a violin-making shop in Michigan in 1890 and five years later began making strings. He's pictured with one of his string-making machines (*bottom, left*) and with co-workers in the violin shop (*opposite;* Squier on right). Strings became the most important Squier product, and Fender bought the company in the 60s. The V.C. Squier **string factory** is pictured (*below, left*) in 1972. Fender adopted the **Squier** name for a new line of guitars made in Japan in 1982, like this Strat (main guitar), at first sold only in Europe, and with Fender and Squier Series logos. Two of the new Squiers are seen at the **UK launch** (*below*).

company around the time of the CBS sale to form the GHS string firm in the same town). Seven years later, in 1972, CBS moved V.C. Squier and its 100 employees to a new location within Battle Creek, and later renamed it the Fender Strings Co.

Steve Squier, who is a distant blood relative of Victor Squier, compiled much of this information about the Squier family and its musical business. Steve is in his early thirties – almost exactly the same age as the Squier guitar brand – and is one of several amateur guitarists in his family. He doesn't play a Squier at present, although he did once own a Squier bass. "Jerome Bonaparte and Victor Carroll are certainly the ones who brought the most fame to the Squier name," Steve says, "but their work represents a tradition of do-it-yourself musicianship and craftsmanship that has been manifested in a variety of ways throughout the family."[44]

Back at Fender in the early 1980s, the company now had its name for the new budget Japanese line. One consequence of using "Squier" that they did not foresee was the effect it would have on an American musician named Billy Squier. He'd scored a Top 5 album the previous year with *Don't Say No*, as well as two Top 40 singles, and another Top 5 album in summer '82, *Emotions In Motion*. Billy says it was around the middle of 1982 when he discovered that Fender was about to launch a new line of guitars with the Squier name. "Not the familiar S-q-u-i-r-e spelling," he says, "but S-q-u-i-e-r … as in Billy Squier."

He noticed that two of the guitars in the new line were similar to an old Fender Tele and Strat he played regularly. "I had a lot of visibility at the time," explains Squier. "I called my lawyer and asked him to contact Fender and find out what they were up to. Fender claimed to have a long-standing relationship with a string-maker named Vincent Squier and that the Squier line of guitars was named for him. Vincent, it seemed, had very little visibility outside the Fender front office."

Squier and his lawyer suggested to Fender that a random sample of people with an interest in rock music and electric guitars would identify the new Fender Squier series with Billy Squier. "The company would therefore be using my name to promote their product without compensating me accordingly," he says. "We summarily reached an agreement under which Fender paid me to settle any claims I might have against the company regarding the use of the name 'Squier' in conjunction with their new guitar line."[45]

Dan Smith recalls the episode a little differently from Fender's perspective. "Yes, I remember Billy Squier trying to sue us, claiming that we used the Squier name to trade off his tremendous star power. And I remember it really ticked off both Roger Balmer and me that CBS settled at all, when he wasn't even in our thoughts when the Squier name was considered."[46]

There was a further consequence to Fender's choice of a name with an unusual spelling: ever since, the name has been regularly misspelled (usually as "Squire") and sometimes mispronounced. "This is a sore spot for us," Steve Squier, the family's historian, says with a weary smile. "We can say it out loud and spell it out for people, and they will still repeat it back to us wrong. It's pronounced just like "squire", the word for a knight's attendant, and the spelling of the guitar line is the original spelling in our family – I have V.C. Squier's grandfather's autograph from 1836 to prove it. One branch of our blood relatives goes by 'Squires' – because that's what everybody seems to want to call us. But the rest of us stubbornly kept the original spelling."[47]

So, back in the early 80s, the Fender team had the Squier name for its new cheaper series of instruments, with five models in place. These created a new base level of the existing Fender Japan Vintage line, but with the "Squier Series" logo on the ball of the headstock, and all intended for export from Japan to Europe. Just as with the Japan Vintage and planned US models, there were two Stratocasters (a maple-neck '57-style and a rosewood-board '62), a '52 Telecaster, and three basses. (Bass guitars are beyond the scope of this book and will only be mentioned occasionally and in passing.) The first run of these new Fender Squier Series guitars was produced at the Fujigen factory around the end of April 1982, alongside the first of the new Fender Japan models.

Joe Allrich was Fender's export sales manager at the time, and he remembers the specific European agents who took these first Squier Series models. Most important sales-wise was CBS/Fender Ltd in England, which distributed to the UK and Germany and to the Benelux countries (although Mexo Musical Instruments GmbH took over German distribution around this time). The early Squiers also went to Gaffarel Musique S.A. in France, M. Casale Bauer S.p.A. in Italy, Letusa S.A. in Spain, Muskantor Musik AB in Sweden, and A. Marcandella AG in Switzerland.[48]

Around June 1982, the first Fender Squier Series instruments reached the UK and, presumably around the same time, the other European distributors. The first review appeared in the July 10 issue of the British music paper *Melody Maker*, where Paul Colbert was impressed. These were the first examples of the Japanese Fenders that players outside Japan had seen. "They are very, very good," wrote Colbert. "Was a time when you could buy a guitar that looked, played, and sounded like a Strat … or you could buy a Strat. Now even that distinction is waving goodbye. In truth, Tokai are as detailed in their replicas but, psychological or not, having that Fender logo at the top of the headstock puts heritage in your hands, even if given an Eastern interpretation."

This was precisely Fender's intention: it's a copy … but it's a *genuine Fender* copy. It was, quite simply, a brilliant move. Colbert reviewed all five of the new Squiers: he said the '57 Strat "sits right, moves easily under the fingers, and is a pleasure to play"; the '62 Strat was his favourite, "a cracker of a guitar" with a "Pickup Made In USA" sticker on the pickguard. He found the '52 Tele less captivating, describing it as "functional".[49]

CBS/Fender's list prices for the UK pitched the '57 Stratocaster at £223, the '62 Stratocaster at £230, and the '52 Telecaster at £198 (all hovering around the equivalent

1982 Fender Squier Series Telecaster '52 Butterscotch

FENDER + JAPAN = FENDER JAPAN

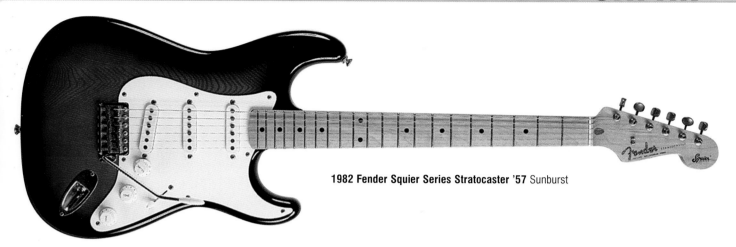

1982 Fender Squier Series Stratocaster '57 Sunburst

■ Two more Fender **Squier Series** models of 1982 are pictured here, made by Fujigen in Matsumoto, Japan. Seen at a **Fender/Fujigen** meeting that year (*opposite, left to right*) are Kousuke Hirabayashi, Ace Nakata, Dan Smith, Ken Kamijo, Bill Schultz, and Johnny Saitoh. **Dan Smith** from Fender planned the new models with Fujigen, here (*right*) showing how to shape a neck. To produce the new guitars, Fender formed **Fender Japan**; pictured at its launch in Tokyo in 1982 (*below, left to right*) are: Masamitsu Yamano (Yamano Music), Bill Schultz (Fender), Chitoshi Kojima (Kanda Shokai), and Roger Balmer (Fender).

of about $400). These prices were almost exactly the same as the cheapest Tokai copies in Britain at the time – and that was obviously not a coincidence. Meanwhile, the list price for the cheapest US-made Fender Stratocaster was £436, which made the Squiers about half the price. As if that wasn't enough, the excellent Squiers offered the only way for a European guitarist to buy a new vintage-look Strat or Tele or bass.

Graeme Mathieson was a district sales manager at Fender's UK distributor at the time, and he recalls the instant and overwhelming success of the new Squier Series guitars. "When they came into the stores, it was unbelievable, absolutely unbelievable. Everybody was prepared to slag them to bits, because it's a Japanese Fender – what's that all about? But when they played them, everybody just said: these are better than the American guitars. It got to the point where we were told as salesmen not to take any more orders, because we had so many on back order – and we weren't selling anything else."

Mathieson remembers a visit to the Hessy's store in Liverpool, one of the most important outlets in the UK at the time. The boss there, Bernard Michaelson, told Mathieson he wanted to order 50 of the new Squier Series Stratocasters. "I thought, I can't take an order for 50 Strats after being told not to take any," Mathieson recalls. "But I said, maple or rosewood? Bernard said oh, they come in both? I'll take 50 of each. And 50 Teles as well. I was leaving the shop with my heart sinking, because I'd taken a great order for 150 guitars – and I was just thinking, well, I'm going to get a right telling-off for this."[50]

The reaction was similar in other European countries, and in Britain there was a distinct buzz about the new Squier guitars, with their unbeatable combination of good value, great playability, vintage vibe, and official Fender association. The main attraction was to players at a semi-pro or amateur level, but pros too were seduced by this particular combination. Mathieson remembers Alan Murphy as a good example of this: Murphy, who worked with Kate Bush, acquired and used one of the Squier Series Strats almost as soon as they appeared.

Within a short space of time after the Squier Series appeared in Europe, Fender decided to make a change to the logos on the headstock of the instruments. Roger Balmer, Fender's head of marketing and sales, recalls a lively meeting with John McLaren, the boss of CBS Musical Instruments. "He practically tore my head off for the idea of 'Fender' on a foreign-made product," Balmer says. "The meeting centred on what to call this line, Squier or Fender, and how we would present that – and so we changed to a large Squier logo. Japanese pressure was one way, for big Fender and no Squier; our position was Squier first, then Fender; and after this meeting with McLaren, it became Squier first. And that was the right decision, I think."[51]

Martin Fredman, who headed up Fender's UK distributor, says: "The trouble with the big-Fender logo, which the originals had, was that it really didn't look much different. The actual guitars, from a design point of view and aesthetic point of view, were the same, so there had to be some differential to make people realise they weren't the authentic

American product, but that they were getting something made under the auspices of Fender – they just wouldn't pay so much money for it."[52]

British salesman Graeme Mathieson recalls that the first two deliveries of the new guitars to Britain had the big-Fender small-Squier logos. "Then the third delivery came in with the big-Squier logo," he says. "We knew that was happening – a running change. It hit the market with the new logo, and everyone said well, it's a shame, but you know what? They're still a great guitar and still great value for money – and we knew we still had loads of people wanting them. It passed over like it never happened." Mathieson reckons maybe 500 big-Fender models reached the UK before the logo change.[53] Steve Preston, who ran the UK service department, estimates there were a few hundred.[54]

Collectors today value these early big-Fender-logo Squier Series models for their rarity and excellence. Ace Nakata, factory manager at Fujigen at the time, is baffled by the interest in this tiny change. "The Squier name was owned by Fender USA," he says, "and any and all changes were ordered by them. Such small details and changes are a regular part of instrument-making, and nobody pays any attention to this at the factory."[55]

The second-batch Vintage models rolled off the Fujigen line around July 1982 and soon reached the European distributors – they were the same guitars but simply had this small change to the headstock logos (although changes would soon be made to wood choice, pickups, and so on). There was now a large "Squier" logo in a vintage spaghetti-like font and in the position where "Fender" had always been. Underneath, in a small line, was "Made In Japan". Under the "Stratocaster" or "Telecaster" model name, which curved around the rest of the headstock to the right, was a "By Fender" logo. This marked the proper birth of the Squier By Fender brand.

That was the story in Europe, at least. Back in Japan – where the Squier guitars were made at the Fujigen factory under the auspices of the new Fender Japan joint-venture between Fender USA and the two Japanese distributors, Yamano and Kanda – an announcement was made in October 1982, this time at a Fender Japan dealer conference at the Hotel New Otani in Tokyo. Present from Fender USA were Schultz and Balmer. "For five months since May this year, we have enjoyed good sales," Balmer told the gathering. "Since our contract manufacturer, Fujigen Gakki, still has much more production capacity, we today announce a new brand, Squier, to help further expand our share on the domestic [Japanese] market."

Schultz told the conference that the new Squier brand was intended to regain market share among younger players that had been lost to video games and other distractions. He also confirmed that Fender was trying hard to block the sale of copy guitars in all territories. "I wish to have the cooperation and support of you, the dealers, to help prevent the sale of these copy instruments and to rid the market of them," Schultz said.[56]

The addition of Squier models to the domestic Japanese market meant that, from late 1982, Fender Japan's Vintage model line-up added one or two layers of cheaper

1983 Stratocaster '62 Fiesta Red

1984 Bullet S-3
3-Color Sunburst

1984 Bullet S-3T
3-Color Sunburst

■ Soon after the arrival of the first Squier models, Fender changed to a large **Squier logo**, as on the Strat here. Sales of the new guitars spread outside Europe (**German ad**, *top*) to Japan, where this **1983 ad** (*opposite, top*) says Squier has "inherited Fender blood". British players took to the new Squiers: **Adrian Murray** (*opposite*) of Iron Maiden plays his modified Squier Strat on stage at Madison Square Garden in 1983. Late that year, Fender decided to sell Squier guitars in the USA. Among the first models were several **Bullets** (guitars *above*), as featured in this **US ad** (*above left*).

Squier models under the existing Fenders. For example, in addition to the existing Fender '57 Stratocasters at ¥65,000, ¥85,000, and ¥115,000, there were now two Squier models at ¥45,000 and ¥50,000. (At the time, ¥45,000 was the equivalent of about $180; ¥115,000 was about $460.)

Collectors today refer to these highly praised early Fender Japan guitars and basses – with the Fender or Squier brand, and wherever they may have been sold – as the JV models, because they bear serial numbers that start with those two letters, which stand for Japan Vintage. An early ad for Squier placed by Fender Japan at the end of 1982 summed up the position well: "Fender blood has now passed to Squier."[57]

With Squier guitars proving a great success in Europe and just launched on the Japanese market, Fender considered the next logical move. Could they sell a made-in-Japan guitar in the United States? Back home, Fender still faced a mountain of problems. They had not yet turned around the factory at Fullerton, and the company was not showing the kind of profit that CBS wanted. Fender boss Bill Schultz was flying back and forth to CBS HQ in New York City for meetings where he fought to keep the company afloat. "We wanted to wait to introduce the Fujigen product to the US market until after we had a solid US-made product line," Dan Smith recalls. "But we were running out of time. So I sold Bill on the concept of using the features from the most disliked Fender guitar for a Japanese-made Squier that we would sell in the USA."

That disliked guitar was the "three-bolt" Stratocaster, a modified standard model introduced by CBS in 1971. As we learned earlier, Smith had only just returned the regular US Strat to the original four-bolt fixing of neck to body. The '71-type three-bolt model had featured a distinctive larger headstock, and it was this style – three-bolt fixing, big headstock – that Fender adopted for the first Squier model to be sold in the USA. Fujigen underlined its reputation for quality by making a good guitar, modifying the original and much-criticised three-bolt joint so that, at last, it provided a sturdy fit.

Fender's plan was to sell enough Squier product to help out with the bottom line, but not so much to jeopardise the precarious status of the US line. "I took out prototypes of the new three-bolt models to a few key dealers across the country," Smith says, "to make certain that we got that balance right. I went to Sam Ash in New York, I went to Chuck Levin's in Washington, to Guitar Center, which at the time was maybe three or four stores – to all the biggest dealers in the USA. They said well, this is nice, we can sell this … but it's probably not going to have that much of an impact on the Fender USA stuff. Boy, were they wrong! Me too. The new Squier series sold like hot cakes. And that's what really made Squier its own brand and what really told us it could *be* its own brand, when we started to market it in the United States."[58]

The Squier big-headstock Strat went on sale in the USA in late 1983 (and in Japan as the Current Stratocaster and the UK as the Popular Stratocaster). There was a Squier Telecaster issued at the same time, which again had a not-especially-vintage look, with an eight-screw pickguard (the '52 Vintage model had the period-correct five-screw guard). On Fender's January 1984 US pricelist, the new Squier Stratocaster was offered with maple neck or rosewood fretboard at $369, with the new Squier Telecaster listed at the same price. By contrast, the cheapest Fender-brand Strat was the $629 hardtail (no trem) US-made Standard Stratocaster, while the cheapest American Tele was the $589 maple-neck Standard Telecaster. No wonder these Squiers sold so well.

Also that year, Fender began to import new budget Squier Bullet models from Japan. Each had a small Strat-style body and a Tele-like neck – the S-3 with three single-coils and the H-2 with two humbuckers. Both would be gone from the line within a year or two. They appeared on that '84 list at $169 for the hardtail S-3 and $199 for the with-trem S-3T and the H-2. Certainly they were cheap, and while they did have a little of the Fender vibe about them, crucially they were not proper Stratocasters or Telecasters and so lacked much appeal beyond beginners. Collectors today often refer to Squiers from this period as the SQ models, because their serial numbers usually start with those two letters.

Fender's first Squier ad appeared in the USA at this time. "An international team of guitar designers and craftsmen gave these new Squier guitars the same light touch and brilliant tone that made the originals the world's most sought-after electric guitars," it said in part.[59] Note the cautious mention of an "international team" rather than a blatant admission of where these guitars were made. Fender was unsure what the reaction might be.

Fender advertised the new Squier line on the new and highly successful MTV channel, which popularised the broadcast on television of non-stop music videos. The voiceover to Fender's ad went like this: "Great musicians have always picked the special sound of Fender. Now it's your turn with Fender's new Squier guitars. The look, the sound, and the quality are everything you'd ever expect. Here's what you'd never expect …" and at this point a big "from $169" appeared on the screen.

As Smith says, they needn't have worried: these first Squier models were an almost instant hit in America. "It taught us, contrary to what the guys believed at Fender six or seven years before, that people would buy Fender guitars with 'Made In Japan' on them," he says. "In fact, I really believe that our introduction of those first Squiers, worldwide and in the USA, was what legitimised buying Japanese guitars."[60]

It's hard to ignore the significance of the move. It began a shift that led to Fender becoming the international manufacturer it is today. Back in 1984, however, the success of the new Squier guitars was undermined by CBS's continuing dissatisfaction with Fender's overall performance. That year, CBS decided to sell Fender. One estimate had put sales of Fender's guitars down 50 percent in the preceding three years. "CBS does not report financial statistics for its division separately," wrote the *San Francisco Chronicle*, "but attributed an $8.3 million Columbia Group operating loss for the third quarter of 1984 in part to 'continued losses in the musical instruments business'."[61] CBS invited offers for Fender, and various groups made bids, including some existing employees. "I

■ Fender advertised the new Squiers on the popular **MTV** channel over the holiday period of late 1983 into '84. The ad (stills, *right*) has a kid noodling on a Squier Strat in a *Fame*-like practice room, trying the quality tuners, seeing an unexpected price flash on the screen, and (naturally) finding fame and the big time.

SQUIER ELECTRICS

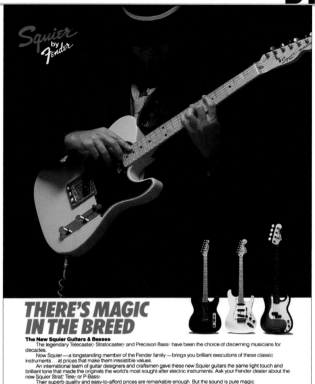

1984 Stratocaster Black

■ Starting in late 1983, Fender began selling in the USA a **Squier Strat** (main guitar), with 70s features including big headstock and 'bullet' adjuster, and a **Tele** (*opposite; ad above*), both of which were highly successful. **Johnny Saitoh** (*above right*) of Japanese firm Fujigen, which made all the early Squier guitars, plays a new Squier Strat in 1983.

was in the process of developing with Fujigen in Japan a complete line of Fender products for sale worldwide," Dan Smith says. "When we put in our bid with CBS, I was going back and forth to try and put this line together – even though we didn't know if we were going to get the company. Fujigen stood by us. They really respected Bill Schultz and the rest of us, so they let us put a product line together. And they made these guitars, not knowing at all what was going to happen." [62]

Bill Mendello was Fender's chief financial officer and part of Bill Schultz's bidding team – along with Smith, Ed Rizzuto, Roger Cox, and Kurt Hemrich. He recalls another way in which the Japanese partners helped. The team had to raise a lot of money but, Mendello says, none of them had any experience of doing so. "Then Bill came up with a great idea: he said let's go talk to Mike Yamano." Masamitsu Yamano was president of Fender's longstanding Japanese distributor, Yamano Music. Like many Japanese businessmen who deal with American firms, Masamitsu adopted a Western forename. Schultz and Mendello flew to Japan, sat down with Mike, and explained the problem.

"Mike looked at us and said: here's a blank cheque; you fill it in. See how much money you can raise – and what you can't raise, I'll make up the difference. Well … when we'd got on the plane to come out to Japan, we felt we probably couldn't buy the company. On the way back, we knew we'd got the financing. We knew we could do it." It's something Mendello will never forget. "Without that, we would not have succeeded. It was that confidence which really made a big difference."[63]

By the end of January 1985, almost exactly 20 years since the corporation had acquired it, CBS confirmed it would sell Fender to "an investor group led by William Schultz, president of Fender Musical Instruments". The contract was formalised in February and the sale completed in March for $12.5 million. This figure compared conspicuously with the $13 million CBS paid for the company back in 1965.

With the hectic months of negotiations behind them, Schultz and his team faced many problems. Probably most pressing was the fact that the Fullerton factory was not included in the deal. American production of Fenders, such as it was, stopped completely in February 1985. The US company employed over 800 people in early 1984. That went down to about 100 by early 1985.

"Scary but exciting" is how Smith described it at the time. "We're not going to be in the position to be able to make any mistakes," he said. "There'll be nobody behind us with a big chequebook if we have a bad month."[64] The new firm established administration headquarters in Brea, California, not far from Fullerton. Six years later, Fender would move admin from Brea to Scottsdale, Arizona, where it remains today.

Looking back now, Smith recalls how he and the team of new owners were desperate to find ways to produce their own guitars on home ground. "We had plans to eventually manufacture again in the USA, but on a small scale," he says. "We actually entertained not manufacturing at all but instead working with a US-based manufacturer on an OEM basis." OEM in this context refers to a company buying in a product from an outside manufacturer and putting its own brand on it. "Bill Schultz and I met with the Heritage crew at the old Gibson plant, but that couldn't be worked out because of the high cost of the product. We also met with Robert Godin up in Montreal, but that deal fell through as well. We even had some ex-employees try to put together a factory, but that fizzled out."

The Japanese operation became Fender's lifeline, providing much-needed product to a company that had no US factory. Every guitar in Fender's 1985 catalogue was made in Japan. Production there was based on Smith's handshake agreement with Fujigen that it would continue to supply Fender and Squier-brand guitars after CBS left the picture. One estimate put as much as 80 percent of the guitars that Fender USA sold from around the end of 1984 to the middle of 1986 as made in Japan.

Eventually, the new team did set up their new US factory. They had machinery from the purchase plus some stockpiled parts. They found a 14,000-square-foot building in Corona, about 20 miles east of the defunct Fullerton site, and started production on a limited scale toward the end of 1985. "Initially we only produced vintage reissue guitars – fewer than ten a day," Smith says. "We thought we would gradually build up to 150 or so a day over a five-year period. We still had Fujigen, who at one point were producing over 10,000 guitars a month for us, and we naively thought that would go on forever. The weakening of the dollar and the strengthening of the yen would change all that."[65] At the end of 1984 the yen stood at around 250 to the US dollar; by the end of 1986, it was half that. It meant that Japanese guitars were becoming too expensive.

In a January 1985 report issued to dealers and in that all-Japanese 1985 catalogue, Fender set out the specifics of what it described as an "exciting new range" of models, notably marking the debut of the Fender and Squier Contemporary series, guitars that "strongly address current players' needs and desires". In other words, these were the company's first nod toward the ever-more-prevalent superstrats – as popularised by Jackson, Charvel, Ibanez, and others – with an early show (for Fender) of humbucking pickups on a regular Strat body.

The report detailed four new Squiers, replacing the earlier models. Some were made by Fujigen, others by Moridaira. They were: the Contemporary Stratocaster, with one or two humbuckers; the Standard Stratocaster, a regular small-headstock Strat, to replace the 1983 big-head model, with maple neck or rosewood board; the Standard Tele, also to replace the '83 model, and with maple or rosewood board; and the Katana, a Squier version of a peculiar new Fender with an offset-V shaped body.

As the 80s progressed and the new owners found their feet, Bill Schultz hinted at plans to move to other overseas sources, telling a trade magazine that Fender would rely on "an international manufacturing strategy".[66] As far as the main markets outside Japan were concerned – primarily North America and Europe – the last Japanese-made Squiers were

1988 Contemporary Stratocaster Torino Red

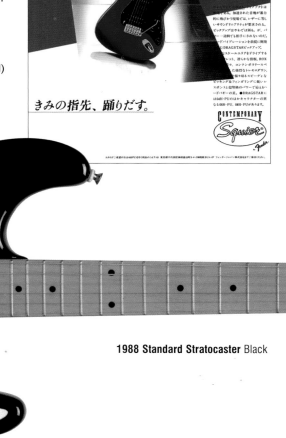

■ In the mid 80s, there were a few new **Japanese** Squier models, including a **Standard Strat** with string-clamp ('axe kickers' ad) and the strange **Katana** (white guitar, *opposite*). By 1988, production of Squiers shifted to **Korea**, because it was too expensive to make them in Japan. There was a trend for superstrat features, as with the Contemporary models (*above,* and ad, *right*), alongside regular Teles and Strats (*below*). An experiment in India failed – **Dan Smith** is seen rousing workers at the Greeta factory (*opposite*) – and the planned **Squier II** guitars ('decisions' ad) moved to Korean production.

1988 Standard Stratocaster Black

Squier releases 10 axe kickers.

Once you test drive one of Fender's Squier® guitars, you're going to kick your old axe goodbye.

Because the Squier Stratocaster®, Telecaster® and Bullet® guitars and the P-Bass®, J-Bass® and Bullet® basses offer you the sound and quality you'd expect from Fender — at unbelievable prices starting at less than $400.

But price is not the main reason to check out a Squier. *These axes kick.*

To find out more about Squier guitars and basses, see your Fender dealer.
Sole Distributor in Australia:
Fender Australia Pty Ltd
13-15 Pemberton Street
Botany, NSW 2019
(02) 666-3929

Squier by *Fender*

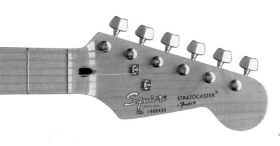

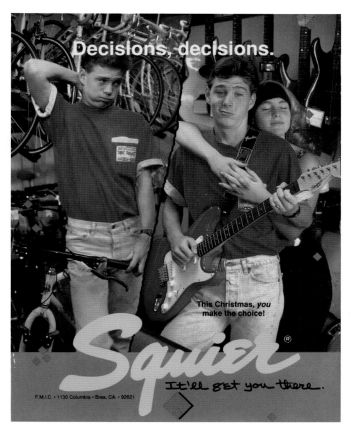

Decisions, decisions.

This Christmas, *you* make the choice!

Squier®
It'll get you there.

F.M.I.C. • 1130 Columbia • Brea, CA • 92621

sold in 1987 and 1988. In Japan itself, as we shall see, the homegrown Fenders and Squiers continued, and indeed blossomed. Fender USA continued to import some Japanese-made Fender-brand models and would use Japan again for Squier on a handful of later occasions. But for now, the Japanese Squier connection was at an end for the international market. Korea was the new source intended to replace Japan, as Fender put behind it the unsuccessful Samick-made Bullet experiment of a few years earlier.

Korean Squiers first appeared around 1988, and most – an assortment of Standard, Contemporary, and H.M. models – leaned toward the superstrat formulas. "We needed to be more than a 'vintage' guitar company," Smith says. "This product was designed to appeal to a wider variety of players, with more modern features better suited to the music that was being played."

Fender's American salesmen had been moaning to management that they had nothing to compete with the "shredder" models from Ibanez, Kramer, Jackson, and the like. "This was a sore point with me," Smith says, "because, after a few less than successful tries, it was clear that the market viewed Fender's attempts as contrary to our image. But we decided to try once again with Squier. By this time, we were working with Cort in Korea, and they conveniently had a series already in production under their own brandname that they could tweak slightly and add quickly to the Squier line-up. We brought over prototypes and hashed them out with a few guys selected from the sales force – and the Squier H.M. series was the result."[67]

The five H.M. models had sculpted bodies and the fashionable appointments of the superstrat style in various combinations. The H.M. I, II, and III appeared in 1989 and were bolt-ons with regular two-pivot trems, the I and II with a bridge humbucker and two single-coils and the III a single-coil in the middle of two humbuckers. The I was the only model of the five variations without a locking nut and a bar string-guide on the headstock. The IV and V were launched the following year and were through-necks with locking trems, both with a single-coil in the middle of two humbuckers, and the V was distinguished by an attractive figured-wood top. Meanwhile, Fender tried another new brand, Heartfield, for a line of Japanese-made superstrats, launched in 1989. As with Squier, the separate brand kept them safely away from Fender, but despite a good deal of marketing effort, the Heartfields were dropped by 1993 and the brand was dead.

Brad Townsend had worked for Fender for a few years from 1978 and rejoined the company in 1984 as a salesman. He recalls that during his stint as vice president of international sales, Fender used three Korean factories: Young Chang (which had connections to the Japanese Moridaira firm), Cort (also known as Cor-Tek), and Samick. "Sometimes the guitars for the domestic market would come from one factory and the guitars for international sales would be produced by another," Townsend recalls. "Sometimes one factory would have a quality issue or a delivery issue – since Fender wasn't their only customer – and we would move production out of one into another. But eventually, Fender would end up doing business with that factory again, because there were basically only the three good factory choices."

Changes like this to the sources of guitars meant that it could be difficult to ensure consistency. Fender had used a system since the 70s for identifying specific models by allocating each one a unique ten-digit 'part' number. "But sometimes when models shifted from factory to factory or even country to country, they might keep the same part number," Townsend says. "This became a real nightmare when it came to customer service, since the factory origin of the guitar had to be identified in order to supply the correct spare parts. As an example, there was no standardisation of things like screw-hole placements on pickguards. Each factory drilled the holes wherever they felt they should go. So if a customer decided to purchase a replacement pickguard, or needed a warranty replacement, the holes didn't line up. That situation went on for many years."[68]

Fender made a brief attempt to produce guitars in India, at the Greeta factory in Madras (now Chennai), around 1988, adopting the Squier II and Sunn brandnames for the budget-conscious results. The Indian guitars – a couple of Strat variants – were of inconsistent quality. One insider remembers that Fender destroyed more of them than it shipped. A letter to dealers dated September 1988 apologised for the mess, saying that "supply is going to be drastically less than what we had planned". Later Squier II models were made by Samick in Korea, some through a deal with Texas-based distributor IMC, but all were gone by 1992.

Squier's July 1989 pricelist showed the following models, all made in Korea: two Squier II Strats, with regular pickups ($199.99) or bridge humbucker plus two single-coils ($219.99); one Standard Strat with maple or rosewood board, and one Standard Tele ($319.99); three H.M. models – I, II, or III – with various pickups and trems ($319.99, $399.99, $499.99); and one Contemporary Strat ($379.99).

Squier settled down to Korean manufacture, but by now an alternative had presented itself, this time closer to home. CBS had used Mexican firms for packing and making strings, but when the new owners took over, a Fender engineer, Bashar Darcazallie, went to Mexico and set up low-key manufacturing there in a converted church in Ensenada, in 1987. Ensenada is about 180 miles south of Los Angeles, just across the California–Mexico border, about a three-hour drive from the Corona factory. With that facility running successfully and making some electronics, it seemed logical to make guitars there, as well.

Fender enlisted the help of Fujigen, and the two firms set up a joint venture, F&F, to develop a guitar manufacturing facility at Ensenada. Key people came over from Fujigen's plant in Japan and trained the workers at the new Mexican guitar factory, modelling the processes and layout on the factory back in Matsumoto. Bill Mendello remembers the transition. "Fujigen brought their machinery with them, plus five or six people. We opened up our Mexican operation, and Fujigen trained the people, using their techniques. So the manufacture of guitars in Mexico was more Japanese-like than it

1990 H.M. V Antique Burst

It'll get you there.

Get ready for a new Classic.

From a team of international designers, musicians and craftsmen comes Squier—a quality line of guitars, basses and amplifiers for everyone. So compare sound, compare fit-and-finish, compare prices. You'll discover Squier *means* unbeatable value.

Introducing the next legend... **Squier**

1989 H.M. II Midnight Wine

46

■ Squier adapted a line of superstrats made by **Cort** in Korea under its own brand to create the **H.M.**s, launched in 1989 (II and V shown, plus a snap of a crackle-finish III, *opposite*).

Elsewhere, Squier pushed the **Contemporary** ('new classic' ad) and discovered graffiti and skateboarding (1989 ad, *opposite*). The **1987 catalogue** (*below*) had an uncertain selection

of superstrats, regular models, and hybrids of the two. British pros continued to discover Squiers: here **George Harrison** plays a Strat (*above*) on stage for the Prince's Trust in 1988.

Squier by Fender

Players have long admired the legendary sound and feel of Fender guitars and basses. Squier—a long-standing member of the Fender family—brings you brilliant executions of those instruments at remarkably affordable prices.

The design and production of the Squier line of instruments is supervised by Fender's master craftsmen. Everything from the selection of quality hardwoods, to the winding of pickups, right down to the final setup must meet Fender's demanding specifications. The final result is brilliant sound, superior playability and solid, dependable quality.

So that you can choose an instrument that matches your playing style, the Squier lineup offers guitars with various pickup configurations, tremolo systems and body shapes.

The widely imitated and instantly recognizable Fender headstock and neck comes with maple or rosewood fretboards. And adjustable bridges and truss rods make them easy to set up for different string gauges and playing styles.

High gloss, durable finishes are available in: Black (506), Arctic White (580), Torino Red (558), Lake Placid Blue (502) and Blonde (501).

was US-like. We had a few people from the USA help them, but for the most part the training, the techniques, the painting – all were Japanese."[69]

Nick Sugimoto was part of the Fujigen team. "We were especially involved in developing the painting of guitars," he says, "because the environmental objections were under way in California. Fujigen was very good at using polyester, so we got together to build up the paint shop and also the assembly shop in Ensenada."[70]

With this level of training, the Mexican workers soon became adept and skilled, and by 1991 the first guitars appeared from the plant – the Fender Standard Stratocaster and Telecaster – while the first Mexican Squier models were launched in 1993, including a regular Strat and Tele plus (briefly) a Floyd Rose Stratocaster, equipped with the vibrato of that name. "The original plan," Dan Smith says, "was for Mexico to make products for export to the USA and other parts of the world, plus a lower-priced line of product for the Japanese market. This was Fujigen's plan for combating the production being lost by Japan to Korea."

In fact, the partnership with Fujigen did not last. "The product Mexico manufactured for the Japanese market didn't meet the price-points they were attempting to hit," Smith says, "and the quality was not initially good enough for the Japanese market."[71] Fender bought out Fujigen's interest and (very successfully) continued alone to develop the Mexico plant. In the years that followed, the Mexico factory would become an important part of Fender's manufacturing capability, including the production of some Squier models. What many people don't realise is that it wouldn't have happened at all were it not for some essential help from the Japanese at its birth.

Meanwhile, Fender's attitude to its relatively new brand appeared to be wavering. One of the fundamentals of the Squier brand until now had been that it was applied to guitars made outside the USA – which so far meant Japan or Korea, if you ignore the Indian dalliance. However, in the early 90s, a Squier Stratocaster appeared with "Made In USA" on the headstock. It was one of no fewer than four variants of the Mexican-made Standard Stratocaster: the regular made-in-Mexico Fender-brand Stratocaster, launched in 1991; a made-in-USA Fender for sale in Japan only; a regular made-in-Mexico Squier, launched in 1993; and this unusual made-in-USA Squier model, which appeared around 1991.

George Blanda, who worked in Fender's R&D department at the time, explains how it worked. "Corona-made bodies and necks were sent to the Mexican factory for painting and buffing. Pickguard assemblies were then added to the made-in-Mexico versions, with pickups by Cort and bridges and tuners by Ping. For the made-in-USA versions, the painted bodies and necks were shipped back to Corona for final assembly. The standard for labeling a product 'Made In USA' is that more than 50 percent of the value must be from the USA and the final transformation – the assembly – must be done in the USA. So, of course, the US-made Squiers fit these criteria. They lasted only about a year and were never big sellers. The Mexican-made model was redesigned in early 1991 to use Corona-stamped pickguards and metal parts plus Corona-designed and Mexican-made pickups. We also added Telecasters."[72]

Early in 1992, the Squier line portrayed in the US pricelist was as follows (all Korean-made but one): one Squier II Strat Contemporary (bridge humbucker plus two single-coils) and one Standard (three single-coils) $249.99; one Standard Strat and one Standard Tele $319.99; five H.M. superstrats $389.99–$759.99; three Floyd Rose superstrats $439.99–$499.99; and the made-in-USA Strat, called the U.S. Standard, at $499.99. The cheapest Fender-brand Strat at the same time was the $399.99 Mexican-made Standard model, and the cheapest Tele, also a Mexican Standard, listed at $389.99.

Another sign of Fender's uncertainty about Squier's relationship to the mother brand came in 1992, when a line of made-in-Korea Strats and Teles appeared with a large Fender logo and a small "Squier Series" logo on the tip of the headstock. "For musicians who want the quality and performance of a Fender guitar but don't think they can afford it, the Fender Squier Series is the answer," ran the press blurb, noting that the Strat had a list price of $289.99. Around 1994, they were replaced with similar made-in-Mexico versions. The big-Fender small-Squier approach echoed the 1982 Japanese guitars that had first set the Squier story in motion – although this incarnation of the Squier Series was without the crucial original combination of high quality and a vintage vibe. The Mexican ones were dropped by the middle of 1996.

A further signal of Squier's poor visibility on the Fender radar in the early 90s was that from around early 1993 to late 1995 the only big-Squier-logo guitars on the catalogue were a pair of Korean Strats (one with the regular three single-coils, the other with bridge humbucker and two single-coils). No Teles, no superstrats – nothing apart from the big-Fender Squier Series. It was almost as if the brand had been swept under the carpet.

Some more brief oddities at this time were Japanese-made Squier Strats and Teles sold only in Britain and Japan and called the Silver Series. For some guitarists, they marked a return to Japanese quality amid the unexceptional Squiers of recent years. There was a rosewood-board or maple-neck Strat (plus a Special Strat with humbucker) and a single maple-neck Tele, all in a range of colours and known in the UK as the Silver Series Stratocaster and Silver Series Telecaster (in Japan as the SST-33 and the STL-33) and all with a small "Silver Series" on the headstock tip. There was also a related Hank Marvin signature model in the UK, but without the Silver Series logo, and a Japanese-made Wayne's World Strat, tied in to the successful movie, which was sold in the States and elsewhere. Launched in 1992, they were all shortlived.

One Silver Series Strat will probably hold the record for some time as the world's most expensive Squier. It was sold at auction in 2003 as an ex-George Harrison and ex-Spike Milligan guitar for the remarkable sum of $29,384. Other non-celebrity examples tend to sell for rather less.

1993 Silver Series Telecaster Sunburst

1993 Silver Series Stratocaster Torino Red

SQUIER ELECTRICS

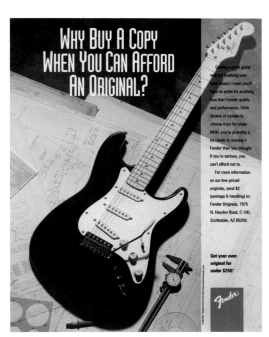

WHY BUY A COPY
WHEN YOU CAN AFFORD
AN ORIGINAL?

■ There was a brief return to export Japanese production in 1992 with the **Silver Series** models, for sale in the UK as well as Japan. Shown are a Tele and Strat, as well as a stylish catalogue (*above*). From 1992 to '96, a Strat and Tele made in Korea and then Mexico recalled the first Squiers, with **large Fender** and small Squier Series logos (Strat head, *below*), while an **ad** (*left*) stressed how these gave Squier an edge over the copyists.

With overseas sales otherwise at a halt, Japanese-made Squiers ebbed to a trickle in Japan itself. The joint venture continued: Yamano and Kanda Shokai sold imported Fender products on the Japanese market and supplied Fender-brand guitars for export to America and elsewhere. But the line they offered at home often differed from that available in other territories, because Fender Japan was free to determine which models to produce and sell to meet the particular demands of Japanese customers. Fender Japan's domestic catalogue of 1991, for example, boasted a typically big range, including Japanese-made Fender-brand reissues not available elsewhere at the time, such as a '54-style Stratocaster, '62 and '72 Telecasters, and a '75 Deluxe Tele.

A year or so into the joint venture, Fender Japan's director, Iwao Saito, told a trade magazine how the partnership was developing. "In the beginning," he said, "we followed Fender's methods heavily. However, it is not so much of a one-sided relationship any more. These days, Fujigen, the manufacturer in Japan, and Fender are exchanging know-how. This benefits both sides and starts to build an ideal business relationship. We are sending out many product ideas to America, and sometimes, based on these ideas, new products are born."[73]

At Fender HQ in the USA, there was a growing feeling that Fender Japan was going its own way. Of course, the Japanese market was different and required a different approach. There was, for example, the country's finely layered pricing system, with small increments between one model and the one above or below it. A myriad of subtle differences meant the product line grew rapidly.

Fender USA was supposed to have control over the new models that Fender Japan made and sold. But as Dan Smith recalls, when he visited the country he'd often find himself in a store flicking through the latest catalogue with some dismay. "I'd see 17 new models that we were never asked about. Part of my job," he smiles, "was to be a policeman for what Fender Japan was doing."

There was a good reason for this, from the American perspective. "We were finally getting the US manufacturing up and going," Smith says, "and we didn't want Japan to make copy models of our stuff. We still wanted to sell US-made guitars in Japan. So we tried to put some controls in place. But we also had to make sure that the product line that they did sell was competitive. It was a real juggling act."[74]

Fender's management was in receipt of some further important fiscal help from the Japanese. As part of their financial arrangements, the new owners of Fender – Schultz and his team – had borrowed from a venture capital company, who in return claimed 49 percent of the shares, with the right to sell those back to the owners in five years. In 1990, with the five years up, the venture capitalists were at Fender's door. Bill Mendello, Fender's chief financial officer at the time, recalls what happened. "True to their word, they said OK, we want our money out, and they put the 49 percent of the shares to us. We needed to pay them off – and as a growing company we didn't have the financing to do that.

They put us in a situation that, once again, could have forced us to sell the company." Schultz and Mendello went once more to Yamano and Kanda Shokai. "Bill Schultz and I and Yamano and Kanda put cash into it – and most of the cash came from the Japanese – so that we were able to pay off the company," Mendello says. "So again, five years later, at a very critical time – a time when most people don't know that Fender very easily could have been sold out from under us – the Japanese and their financial ability saved the company. That's something you never forget."

Mendello agrees that, inevitably, the Americans and the Japanese had their differences over the years. "But for the most part they were very minor differences, and all of us wanted to do what was best for ourselves but at the same time do what was best for Fender. If I look back at why Fender was successful, Mike Yamano is one of the three or four key people. You look at myself, at Bill Schultz, at Dan Smith, and you look at Mike Yamano, and maybe someone at Kanda Shokai – and the list goes down from there."[75]

US pricelists for 1995 had a Korean Squier Bullet Standard Strat ($239.99) and a Korean Squier Standard Strat ($249.99). The January '96 list had the last show of the Mexican Fender Squier Series Strat and Tele ($309.99). The cheapest Fender-brand guitars at this time, other than those Squier Series anomalies, were the Mexican Fender Standard Strat and Tele, each at $409.99.

Fender wanted still cheaper Squiers, and from 1995 China became the new source, followed a year or so later by Indonesia. The Chinese deals were made through Reliance, based in Taiwan, which had set up factories across China. Reliance began in 1979 and describes itself as one of the largest musical-instrument OEM corporations in the world. (OEM, or original equipment manufacturer, is where an outside producer supplies goods to a company that puts its own brand on them.)

The first Chinese factory that Fender used for Squier was Yako, based in Zhangzhou in south-east China, about 250 miles east of Hong Kong. Yako was established in 1993, and company records show that it received its first Squier order in May 1995, delivered in August, for 2,000 Squier Stratocasters with rosewood fingerboard (known variously as the Bullet, Traditional, or Affinity model). The first Indonesian Squiers were supplied specifically for the Squier Strat Pak, of which more later. China and Indonesia soon became important sources for Squier, with factories such as Yako, Axl, and Dalian Dongfang in China (and more recently Grand Reward), and Cort and Samick in Indonesia.

Joe Carducci is a Fender veteran – he's worked for the company since 1973. In the early 90s he assisted Dan Smith in managing the guitar product lines, and in 1994 he became marketing manager for imported electric guitars. Fender decided to give Squier the status of an independent product line in 1996 and to appoint for the first time a separate Squier marketing manager. Carducci was the obvious candidate for the job. He sat at his new desk and surveyed the landscape. "The mindset was that Squier was an entry-level

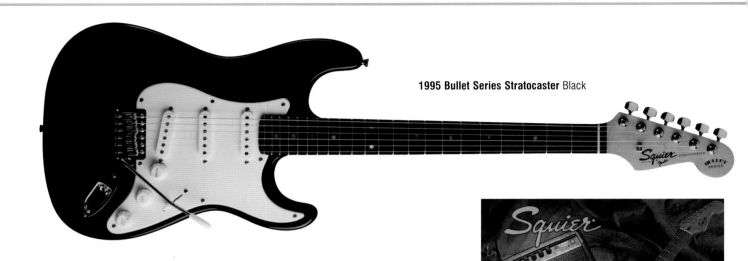

1995 Bullet Series Stratocaster Black

■ So far, Squier's role had developed as Fender's budget brother, made overseas and sold internationally. Around 1991, a loophole meant that a few Squiers were marked **"Made In USA"**, like this special Strat (main guitar) presented to Larry Thomas, now Fender's CEO but at the time working for Guitar Center. Regular examples had a serial number on the headstock (*far right*). Production began in China in 1995 (**Chinese Strat** ad, *right*, and Bullet Series Strat, *above*) while Squiers continued to please beyond beginners: **Jeff Healey** (*far right*) plays slide on a modified Strat.

SQUIER ELECTRICS

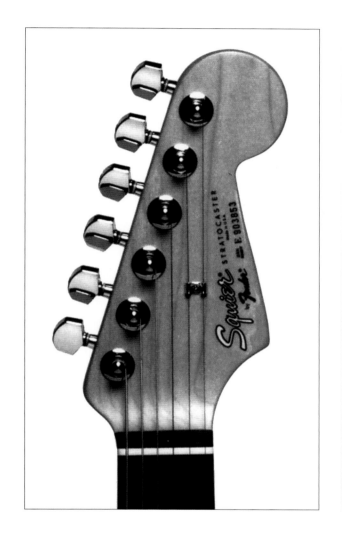

1991 U.S. Standard Stratocaster Black

guitar, and that's it," he recalls. "No frills, just the basics." Carducci's plan, in league with senior management, was to take Squier up a notch or three. As we've seen, Squier had been useful to Fender in more or less disposing of the competition that came from blatant copy guitars, but in recent years its purpose had become unclear, and in the first half of the 90s it looked close to collapse. Fender's opponents now competed in the low-price market by offering more features, better woods, and more colours and finishes. It seemed like a good idea to revive Squier with new purpose and a fresh direction.

"When I entered into the picture, the Chinese Squier Strats and Teles had laminated-plywood bodies 40mm deep," Carducci recalls. "Our competitors were offering solid-ash full-depth 44mm bodies with plenty of colour options. Within the world of Fender, Squier was like the stepchild – Squier guitars didn't have all the cool factor that the Fender models had. That made sense: if you want those features with a famous name on it, you pay more. But our competitors were attacking the Squier brand by offering all those options at the same price-points where Squier lived. We determined that Squier was slowly losing market share to them." Carducci also discovered that entry-level guitar buyers have little or no brand loyalty. The guitar with the set of features that seemed most professional at the best price usually won the sale.

Carducci completely changed the Squier line-up during 1996 and 1997 with revised and new models. He divided them into four series: Tradition or Traditional (renamed Affinity from the start of '97); Standard; Pro Tone (which was very nearly called Deluxe); and Vista. The Affinity and Standard were more or less what had gone before: cheap, basic Strats and Teles. The Korean-made Pro Tones, however, were a clear step up, and the Japanese Vistas were something else altogether.

To ensure a safe birth for the Pro Tone models, Carducci travelled often to the Cort factory in Korea. Designs were drawn up at Fender admin HQ in Scottsdale, Arizona, and sent out to Korea. "Once they made the prototypes," Carducci says, "I went out there at the tail end, to make sure that the fingerboard radiuses were correct for the neck shapes, that the outer edges and the body contours were right – basically making sure all the details were very Fender-like. That wasn't always the case with some of the Squiers that had gone before. The idea with the Pro Tones was to ratchet up the quality, so that when you held one in your arms it felt 'Fender'."

The Pro Tone models were launched in 1996: five classic Strats with features such as ash body, gold hardware, transparent finishes, aged hardware, shell pickguard, and matching headstock, in various mixes; plus a bridge-humbucker Fat Strat, a Tele Thinline, and a neck-humbucker Fat Tele, all with similarly upscale appointments. (These were the first Squiers to use the name 'Fat' for a model with two single-coils and a humbucker at the bridge; a few years later, Double Fat was added, for a model with two humbuckers. Similarly appointed Fender-brand guitars adopted these names at the same time.) The new Squier Pro Tones listed between $499.99 and $639.99, and many players spotted a bargain: these were great-playing and good-looking guitars at keen prices. Sharp-eyed guitarists who were able to stop playing the Pro Tones for a few minutes also noticed some interesting stuff on the headstocks. The Squier logo was rendered in a font that harkened back to the spaghetti-style look of the classic vintage Fenders, while the "By Fender" line underneath was changed from the usual logo-style Fender to simple block capitals. "That was a conscious decision," Carducci says, "so that the Squier logo was the badge of honour, instead of implying that it was the badge of dishonour. It was all done to help Squier stand on its own, to give it its own identity."

The logical extension of that idea would surely have been to remove the "By Fender" line altogether. "We did entertain that idea," Carducci says, "but because Squier shares the same headstocks as Fender and uses the same names – Stratocaster, Telecaster, and so on – we made sure that we put 'By Fender' next to the Squier decal, not so much to add credibility to Squier, but for trademark protection. If the Fender name wasn't there, there are some technicalities where somebody could say, well, we can use those names because you're not protecting them."

Unfortunately, the Squier Pro Tone guitars failed because they succeeded. How can that be possible? "The Pro Tone series was globally accepted," Carducci says, "and certainly served its purpose exactly as we discussed and planned and intended. But ultimately there was a backlash, because they were so good that we were losing sales from our Mexican-made guitars." On the January 1997 pricelist, the basic Mexican Fender-brand Standard Strat or Tele was marked at $429.99 and the Floyd Rose Standard Strat was $519.99 – actually a little less than the more attractive Squier Pro Tones, but it was the Pro Tones that got the attention, if not the big sales. "We did too good a job," admits Carducci. Sales were disappointing and unsold stock built up in Fender's warehouses. The Pro Tones were gone from the catalogue by 1998.

A further innovation from Carducci came with the Squier Vista series. He thought of it as painting outside the line. Others just thought wow, new shapes! Or, at least, new takes on some different shapes. Whichever way you looked at it, it was another brave move. The Fender brand was known for Strats and Teles, and whenever it had tried to stray from the blueprint – the attempt to absorb superstrat-like flavours was a recent example – no one much cared for the results. But in 1996, Fender had released the Jag-Stang, based on the guitar that the late Kurt Cobain had devised with Fender's Custom Shop. "That certainly sent a message loud and clear in the industry that a guitar doesn't have to be a Strat or a Tele to sell. The Fender Jag-Stang also proved that there was a whole generation of guitarists out in the world who didn't necessarily want to play guitars that looked like their dads' guitars," Carducci says.

A plan unravelled to devise new Squier models that, like the Jag-Stang, would offer alternatives to Strats and Teles. Carducci hit upon the Vista name while he worked late in the office one night, trying to think of a new family name for the proposed models. "A

1996 Pro Tone Fat Strat Black

1996 Pro Tone Stratocaster
Vintage Blonde

58

■ The **Pro Tone** Series, introduced in 1996, marked a major step up for Squier in presence and quality. The three examples pictured show how the Korean-made line mixed upscale visuals and finish with good playability. A **1996 ad** (*opposite, bottom*) has the three revised Squier series: Chinese-made Traditional (soon renamed Affinity); Korean-made Pro Tone; and Mexican-made Standard. Squier shouted about the new models, especially the Pro Tones, offering a vibrant **'96 catalogue cover** (*below*) and ads with players such as **Tom Principato** (*above*). But Fender worried that the Pro Tones were so good they were competing with Fender-brand models, and they were removed from the line during 1998.

1996 Pro Tone Thinline Tele
Crimson Red Transparent

vista is a particular vantage point," he explains. "With these new guitars, you had a different vantage point, and you were looking at guitars that were not Strats or Teles."

The ideas for the three Vista designs – the Jagmaster, the Venus, and the Super-Sonic – came from a variety of sources. The Jagmaster was prompted by Mike Lewis. In 1995, Lewis had taken over the job of marketing Fender electric guitars from Dan Smith, who moved from Scottsdale to run the R&D department in Corona. Lewis spotted Bush vocalist Gavin Rossdale playing a Fender Jazzmaster that had two humbuckers duct-taped in position. Bush were enormous – they'd scored two Top Five albums and were everywhere. Carducci describes the decision to create a Squier Vista model based on Rossdale's guitar as a no-brainer. "It was such a great body shape," he says. "As for the tone of the original Jazzmaster played loud, we needed to source some real good humbucking pickups that sounded great at high volume."[76] This they did, at the same time adding to the Jagmaster some straightforward controls and a decent vibrato.

In 1995, Courtney Love was rhythm guitarist in Hole. The band had taken a break during their Live Through This tour to prepare and rehearse for a series of headline shows, including Lollapalooza. Billy Bush, guitar tech for Hole's Eric Erlandson on that tour, takes up the story. "I was talking with Chad Zaemisch, tech for Courtney and bassist Melissa Auf der Maur, and we realised that Courtney could be pretty destructive on stage – and that she only had a couple of guitars that were still usable." One was a vintage Jaguar that Eric had found for her, the other an unusual guitar called a Mercury, built by Danny Babbitt and Tim George in Atlanta. "She was really attached to the Mercury – but, that said, it didn't keep her from throwing it into the crowd on a regular basis," laughs Bush. "I figured we ought to get something like the Mercury that she could abuse, and also some of the new reissue Jaguars. Then she could destroy the Jaguars, and we could keep the Mercury intact. We managed to track down the guys who built the Mercury, but they were no longer making guitars."

Bush knew Alex Perez in Fender's artist relations department. He made a call and Perez agreed to help. "We sent the Mercury and Melissa's favourite P Bass to the Custom Shop," Bush recalls, "and they went to work copying them as much as possible. For Courtney's guitar, they basically copied the body, neck, and pickguard from the Mercury, but with some smoothing and contouring to resemble a Strat or Jaguar. She really wanted a combination of the Mercury, a Fender, and a Rickenbacker."

Love's two-pickup Mercury had a set neck, strings-through-body, and, during its life, anything from zero to three controls. "Chad and I decided that it was best if we made Courtney's Fender as bulletproof as possible for the tour, so we had them make it with just one neck pickup and no controls. She loved the warm tone the neck pickup gave, so we had it made so it was just full on, wired directly to the jack." Bush, Zaemisch, and Perez worked on the details, setting the weight and vibe just as Love wanted them. Fender built three custom guitars for the tour, in green, blue, and pink, and later a black one.

"Courtney loved them," Bush says. "It took some convincing to retire the Mercury, but she dug the Custom Shop pieces they built and she played them for years."

Bush says it was a relief to take some of the pressure off Zaemisch. "He would be the unlucky soul who had to dive into the crowd to retrieve the Mercury when Courtney would throw it. He got pretty beat-up a couple of times. But once we got the Venus guitars, he would try to gauge when the time came in the set when she would decide to smash or throw something, and he'd try to swap the Venus for the Jag reissue. If the Venus went in, so did we – if the Jag went in, well … some kid got lucky and got to keep it."[77]

News from the Custom Shop reached Joe Carducci. "They called me and said hey, we've got something here we're working on with Courtney Love, and it's very cool. They knew I was working on some alternative models and thought I'd want a look. When I saw it, I thought instantly it could be something special." Carducci and his colleagues talked to Love about a production Squier version. "But we said that as far as making it marketable to the masses, it would certainly be a good idea if we added another pickup to it – which is how the bridge humbucker on the Venus came about – and we also added a volume control." The Venus was a spectacular member of the new Squier Vista series, along with a Venus XII 12-string that echoed the Rickenbacker vibe (and it had a tone control, too, plus split pickups like Fender's original Electric XII).

The Vista trio was completed by the Super-Sonic, the idea for which came from a picture that Hendrix-fan Carducci had seen. "Jimi was playing a Jaguar upside-down, and I thought: that's got to be a guitar! Obviously, if you literally take a Jaguar and reverse it, it's not very playable. So we took the basic lines of the guitar, but readjusted the lower bout so that you could get playability in the upper register, plus we made it generally smaller. Also, we tilted the humbucker pickup," Carducci says, "not just to Fender-ise it, but to brighten up the bass string and fatten the high E. And we kept saying that, sonically, it's got to sound great at high volume. So we called it the Super-Sonic."

Sadly for such a fine set of designs, made by the ever-vigilant Fujigen factory in Japan, the Vista guitars did not sell as Fender had hoped. They first appeared on Squier's January 1997 pricelist, with the Super-Sonic, Jagmaster, and Venus at a sizeable $699 each and the Venus XII at a whopping $999.99. They were removed from the line during the following year, although the Jagmaster would be revived later when the Vistas attracted something of a minor cult following. There was also a Chinese-made Vista Musicmaster, which revived the old Fender-brand 'student model' name, but this too was shortlived and was gone from the pricelist by 1999.

On reflection, Carducci admits that the Vistas had to be Squiers – and yet that was part of their downfall. It was OK for Squier to paint outside the line, but not Fender. "At that point in time, Fender would not experiment like that," he says. "And if the rage was to make sharp pointy guitars – which Fender has tried to do at various times – and Fender does that and puts the Fender brandname on them, well, they don't sell. That's just

1997 Jagmaster Sonic Blue

SQUIER ELECTRICS

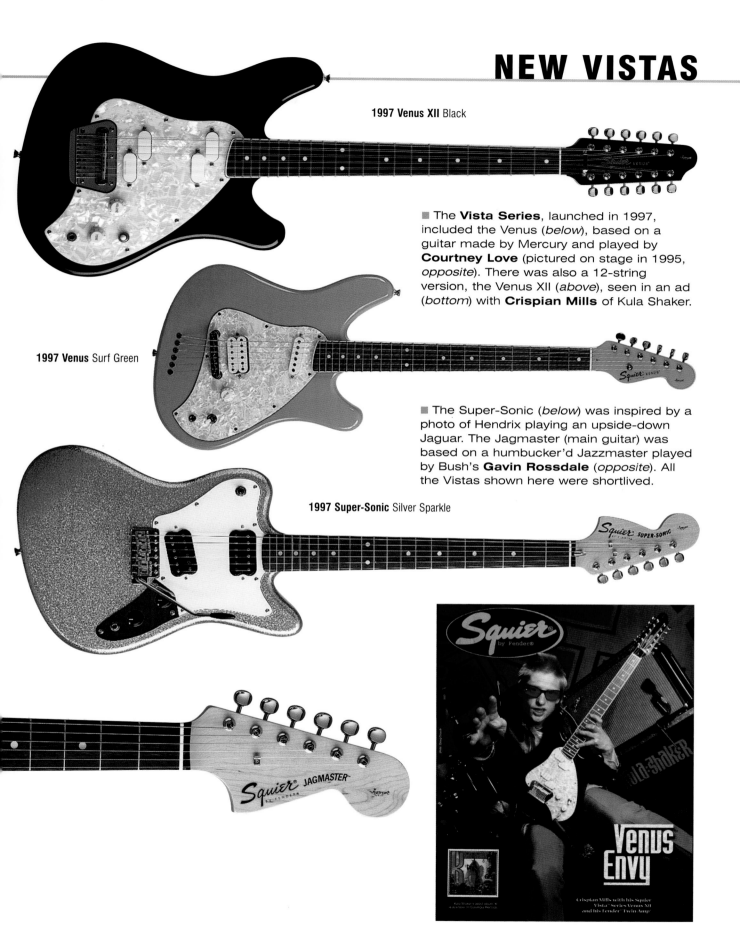

1997 Venus XII Black

■ The **Vista Series**, launched in 1997, included the Venus (*below*), based on a guitar made by Mercury and played by **Courtney Love** (pictured on stage in 1995, *opposite*). There was also a 12-string version, the Venus XII (*above*), seen in an ad (*bottom*) with **Crispian Mills** of Kula Shaker.

1997 Venus Surf Green

■ The Super-Sonic (*below*) was inspired by a photo of Hendrix playing an upside-down Jaguar. The Jagmaster (main guitar) was based on a humbucker'd Jazzmaster played by Bush's **Gavin Rossdale** (*opposite*). All the Vistas shown here were shortlived.

1997 Super-Sonic Silver Sparkle

Venus Envy

Crispian Mills with his Squier Vista Series Venus XII and his Fender Twin Amp history. To make things different and whacky, Fender stayed very conservative in their Strats, Teles, P Bass, and Jazz Bass shapes and designs. Whereas Squier had the image, at that time, to do different kinds of things."

Carducci is proud of the Vistas but disappointed by the way they performed commercially. "We were over-optimistic when we anticipated sales," he says. He describes an imaginary triangle of Fender sales, with small numbers of expensive Custom Shop guitars at the top and large numbers of cheaper guitars down at the bottom. "The Vista series was perceived to live way down there, which led us to believe we had to order in large quantities – whereas what we learned afterward is that, really, because of the price-point, the Vista series lived further up. As the triangle goes up, it gets smaller – so really we shouldn't have ordered so many. But hindsight, as they say, is 20-20."[78]

The Vistas also had the misfortune to hit at a time of faltering sales for the US guitar industry in general. A piece about Fender's Mexican factory in the *Los Angeles Times* in September 1997 put it like this: "The bad news for Fender … is that the guitar market has been flat the last two years after doubling from 1985 to 1995. Indeed, average daily production [of about 420 guitars] in Ensenada is down by one third from two years ago."[79]

Carducci's third Squier innovation, and one that remains a strong part of the Fender line to this day, was the pack concept. Or, as it was rendered in Fender-speak, the Pak. It seems obvious now: take a cheap guitar, a small amp, a cord, a strap, a gig-bag, strings, picks, and a how-to tutor, put them all in a box, and sell it to parents who want to buy the kid a guitar but who know nothing of the subject and would be intimidated in a music store. "We were the first in the world to offer such a thing," Carducci says. "The idea was to make it as easy as possible for mum and dad, with everything in one box."

This 90s innovation was prompted when Carducci went to buy his first home computer. "There were all these accessories, and I didn't know if they were vital. I wasn't sure if the salesman was slowly adding things to take advantage of someone who's naïve. So the computer business started packaging everything in one box. It's your first computer? This is all you need right here to get you going. That's where the mindset came from. Just pick it up and take it to the cash register."[80] The first Squier Strat Pak appeared in 1996, with a Strat and everything else ma and pa might need for the fledgling Jimi. The box of tricks retailed at just $249.99.

A shake-up at Fender resulted in a move for Carducci in 1998. He became purchasing manager, a job that included sourcing Squier and Fender-brand guitars from overseas factories. In later years, Carducci would become the product specialist at the Fender-licensed Gretsch brand, where he still works today.

Mike Lewis had started at Fender in 1991; four years later, he took over from Dan Smith as head of marketing Fender electric guitars. When Carducci moved to purchasing in '98, Lewis took direct control of Squier for a few years. "I basically rolled it back down to a much more simplified range. I'm the one who discontinued all that stuff," Lewis laughs. He's referring to the fact that Squier dropped the Pro Tone and Vista series. To Lewis, it seemed a natural move. "We had recently built our new factory in Mexico, following a bad fire in 1994, and so I had brought a lot of Fender guitars into what was now our own manufacturing plant. That's why many Japanese guitars disappeared and went into Mexico: the Fender Classic series was made in Mexico, for example. We did a lot of things to bring guitars into our own manufacturing plant."

When he took over Squier and looked at what was available, Lewis saw no clearly defined line where budget-brand Squier stopped and main-brand Fender started. He decided to end the overlapping and to streamline the catalogue. "The Squier Pro Tone series was extremely popular, but some of its price ranges were in the same ranges as the Fenders out of Mexico," he says. "We had a lot of comments from our customers: these are great guitars, but why aren't they branded Fender? So I shifted some of the concepts of the Pro Tone series – a lower-priced, deluxe guitar – into the Fender Deluxe series, which began in 1999 at the Mexico factory." Similarly, some of the ideas that underlined the Squier Vistas – especially the willingness to delve into Fender's past for inspirational styles and features – informed 'new' Fender-brand models such as the Toronado and Cyclone, which appeared in 1998 (and the Cyclone became a Squier model in 2003). The notion that it was hip to absorb the spirit and feel of older Fenders would soon come to define an important Squier model – of which more later.

Put simply, in 1998 and 1999 Lewis reorganised the catalogue to make a more clear-cut linear progression from entry-level Squiers, all the way through the various Fenders, and up to the Custom Shop models. "That meant simplifying the Squier range, which I reduced to just the Affinity and Standard," he says. "Above the Squier Standard, the made-in-Mexico Fender Standards began. The whole thing became much easier to follow, in a good–better–best way."[81]

The Squier pricelist of January 1998 reflected the simpler approach, with the line pruned down to three series. The basic Chinese-made Affinity series had a Strat ($249.99), a Tele ($259.99), and a Duo-Sonic ($229.99), an interpretation of the old Fender student model. The Mexican-made Standard series had a rosewood or maple Strat ($329.99), Fat Strat ($339.99), and Fat Strat Floyd Rose ($459.99), plus a Tele ($339.99). Finally, the Vista series had that Chinese-made Musicmaster ($349.99), while the Japanese-made Vistas, on their last legs, had been reduced in price since their launch, with the Super-Sonic, Jagmaster, and Venus at $499.99, and the Venus XII at $799.99. As usual, there were a few basses as well.

Lewis still had his hands full with the entire Fender line, so in 2000 Keith Brawley was appointed as marketing manager for Squier (his title was vice president of strategic brands). Brawley had started to work at Fender in sales back in 1989 and moved to marketing in 1995, where one of his tasks was to help build a consistent brand identity

■ Squier's **Standard models** were spruced up in the late 90s with brighter colour options, such as this purple Strat (*above*). The new Squier **Strat Pak** (*right*) put everything that a fledgling guitarist might want into a single box, advertised with flair by skateboarder **Remy Stratton** (*opposite*). Squier made **exclusive colour options** for certain distributors, such as this yellow Cyclone (*below*) for Yamano of Japan.

2006 Cyclone Graffiti Yellow

66

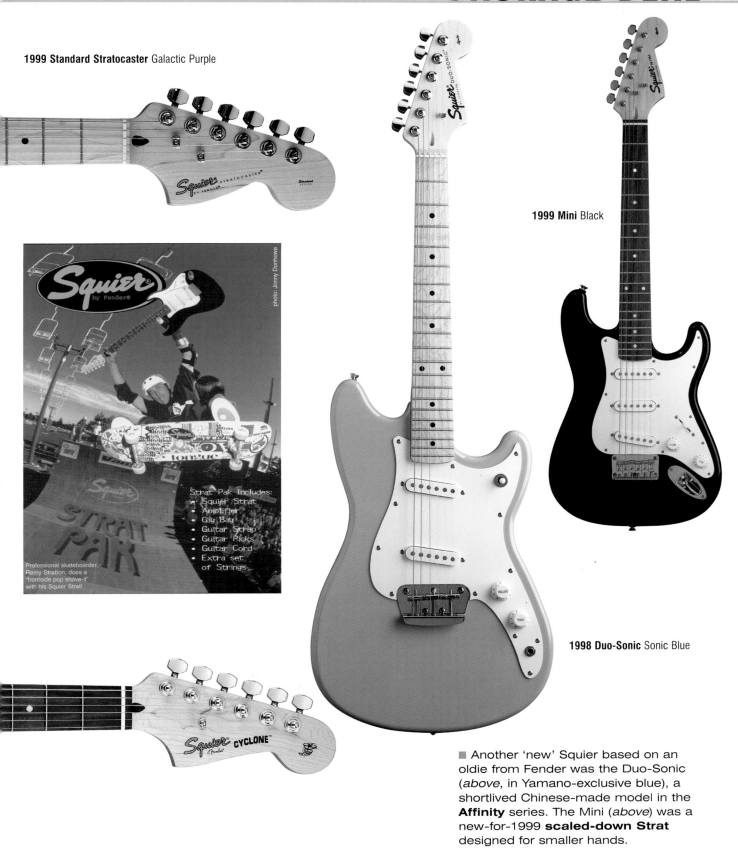

1999 Standard Stratocaster Galactic Purple

photo: Jonny Donhowe

Strat Pak includes:
- Squier Strat
- Amplifier
- Gig Bag
- Guitar Strap
- Guitar Picks
- Guitar Cord
- Extra set of Strings

Professional skateboarder, Remy Stratton, does a "frontside pop shove-it" with his Squier Strat!

1999 Mini Black

1998 Duo-Sonic Sonic Blue

■ Another 'new' Squier based on an oldie from Fender was the Duo-Sonic (*above*, in Yamano-exclusive blue), a shortlived Chinese-made model in the **Affinity** series. The Mini (*above*) was a new-for-1999 **scaled-down Strat** designed for smaller hands.

SQUIER ELECTRICS

for Squier through its ads, sales material, logos, and so on. "The Fender brand, naturally, was the priority of the company up to that point," Brawley says. "But building a portfolio of brands and the strategy that would accompany such a move was not something Fender aimed for at the time."

When Brawley moved to his new job in 2000, he told Bill Schultz that he saw an opportunity to significantly improve Squier instruments without much additional cost – always an attractive business idea. He reckoned that if he could specify exactly what was required to the various factories and take the time to keep them to those specs, the resulting guitars would be better and more successful. "However," Brawley says, "because Squier had always lived in the shadow of Fender, in the organisation, and had been the ultimate responsibility of Fender product managers, it was always, internally, a second-class citizen. But it was the number-one selling brand of electric guitars in the world, in terms of units, so I thought it deserved a vision of its own with dedicated leadership and no handcuffs. Bill enthusiastically agreed."

The first thing Brawley did was to designate certain features as particular to Squier, notably applying slimmer neck profiles to some models than were available on Fender models. Not only did he want to make Squier different from Fender – while retaining the unique value of the original designs – but also he kept in mind that a good part of the market for Squier was younger players, who usually had smaller hands. "I then spent a lot of time in our contracted factories, explaining why we were doing these things," Brawley says, "and how it would benefit them to work closely with me to achieve the goal. The factories all went along with this readily."

The result was some new versions of existing Squier models, which started around 2000 and 2001, with revamped features and, in some cases, changes of factory – although the principal source countries remained as China and Indonesia. Squier also introduced some new takes on the superstrat theme. Brawley says it was all a success, with Squier sales shooting up 71 percent after he re-engineered the line. "A lot of that was attributable to support from the global distribution network. They embraced the changes and enthusiastically threw themselves behind the new products. So the big challenge then became to supply the demand."

The Affinity series remained as the basic, no-frills, entry-level Squier Strat and Tele. Brawley wanted to make a clear gap between that and the first step up, the Standard series. "The Standards seemed to offer the greatest opportunity, and that was where I had a lot of fun," he recalls with a smile. "In contrast to the 'modern oval' neck profile found on the Mexican-made Fender Standard series guitars, I used a 'pencil neck' slim profile from a '68 Stratocaster neck as the template for the Squier Standards. This meant they felt different from Fender, a lot different, and they also felt much different from Affinity models. This was very obvious, very intentional, and instantly recognised by distributors, dealers, and players."

Brawley worked with the factories to improve the Standard pickup specs, moving from cheaper ceramic to better alnico. He encouraged them to develop a hot humbucker, for example, for players who wanted to crank things up. The Fat models were given a 'blackout' treatment of the plastic parts, to add a little more visual attitude, and the line gained a variety of rich metallic colours to supplement the existing Black and Sunburst finishes. The Sunburst finish offered for the Squier Standard had a 60s-like tri-tone effect, for example, which further differentiated it from the Brown Sunburst used on Mexican-made Fender Standard models. All this was developed in what Brawley describes as a skunk works. "It was outside the laborious and corpocratic R&D organisation that was so focused on the Fender brand, and it proved to be critical in getting new product to market quickly and in being responsive to player and dealer feedback."

And then there were the new Squier Stagemasters, "made explicitly with the young rocker in mind," said Fender's press release, "and spelling 'flash' with every feature." They were yet another stab at the superstrat, with distinctive reverse headstocks (designed to provide straight string-pull – or perhaps just to look different) and all the usual distinctions of the style: slim-horned bodies, locking vibrato systems, plentiful finish options including graphics, and the required mixes of humbuckers and single-coils.

All the Stagemaster models were Chinese-made, and there were also some seven-string versions, aimed at the contemporary trend among metalheads for detuning. In quite a few different guises, the Squier Stagemasters lasted from 1999 to 2002, when they were renamed Showmasters following a copyright dispute over the Stagemaster name. Some of the Showmasters limped on to 2005.

There was also an attempt to bolt superstrat qualities to a Telecaster, usually the most resistant model to such advances. The Squier Double Fat Tele Deluxe, launched in 2001, had a carved mahogany body, two exposed-coil humbuckers, and various metallic finishes. The press release described it as a "new spin on a classic guitar design" following in the footsteps of the new Stagemaster line and "designed with today's more edgy guitarist in mind". It lasted a couple of years.

Keith Brawley left Fender early in 2001 to set up his own Brawley Guitars in California. He went on to work at Guitar Center and in 2011 moved to Gibson as president, North America. "Looking back, I'm most satisfied with getting Squier out from under the shadow of Fender," he says, "and getting it established as a line that the company was proud of, rather than one they looked at as a cheap copy brand. I always felt it deserved more than that. And I was able to change the internal culture at Fender, which is probably the hardest thing to do in any company."[82]

Richard McDonald is a long-standing Fender man, at the time of writing senior vice president of marketing and the Fender brand manager. Around 2000, he took on overall responsibility for Squier as part of his job running the Fender brands, and he continued

1999 Stagemaster HSH Frost Red

2001 Double Fat Telecaster Deluxe
Frost Red Metallic

■ Squier was back to the **superstrat** theme in 1999 with the launch of the Stagemaster models (HSH, *top*) with their unusual reverse headstock. The Stagemaster line would evolve into the Showmasters in 2002, but those too would not last long. For the first time with Squier, **humbuckers** turned up on a Tele for the Double

Fat model (*above*) introduced in 2001. **Double Fat** meant two humbuckers, and a **seven-string** Strat (*opposite*) with that layout turned up in 2000 for the metal detuning craze. Squier first offered **T-shirts** in 1999 (*opposite*), and nasty little axe-wielding characters (*right*) populated the 2000 catalogue.

**2000 Standard Double
Fat Strat 7 HT**
Purple Metallic

Squier Logo T-shirts
099-0025
Choice of logo colors on black:
Purple, Orange, Light Blue, Bright Green
M, L, XL, XXL, 3XL
100% cotton, made in the U.S.A

that for the next five years, overseeing Brawley's successor as Squier marketing manager, Mike Tonn, who was hired in early 2001 from the retailer Musician's Friend. McDonald and Tonn worked together to ensure that there was little or no overlap between Squier and Fender models, to avoid the senseless problems that in recent years had led to Squier and Fender more or less competing with one another from within the same company. "They specifically asked me what I would do with the Standard Squier models," Tonn recalls from his job interview, "and I said I would like to shake things up a bit, I'd like to get some different colours in there, that sort of thing. They said well, if you think you can do it, go for it."

Fender also asked Tonn how he would deal with the DeArmond line, left over from Joe Carducci's period. In 1997, Fender's chief financial officer Bill Mendello had announced to Carducci and Mike Lewis that Fender had bought DeArmond, a brand famous since the 40s for pickups and effects-pedals. Mendello asked them for ideas about how to develop the brand beyond those products, and the two came up with a line of Korean-built electrics to represent a less expensive alter ego of Guild, which Fender had acquired in 1995. They were intended to be a kind of Guild equivalent to Gibson's cheaper Epiphone brand, which enjoyed great success. The DeArmond guitar line debuted in Europe in 1998, and in America the following year. Including solidbodies, semi-solids, and archtop electrics, the models were based on well-known Guild designs, some closer to the originals than others and employing similar or identical model names.

The DeArmond line was not the success that Fender had hoped it would be – and now, in 2001, Tonn did not have much room to move to sort it out. His suggestion was to rationalise the DeArmond line and shift it to the Squier brand. "I thought maybe the Squier name would help to give some visibility to the instruments," he says. "I really was at a loss, to be honest. One thing at least I could do was to cull down the number of models." In 2002, the fifteen DeArmond models became seven Squier models: the M-50 and S-65 Indonesian solidbodies, the M-70, M-77, and S-73 Korean solidbodies, and the Starfire and X-155 Korean hollowbodies. Tonn named them the Squier Series 24, because they had a scale-length of twenty-four-and-three-quarter inches, like the Guild originals (and unlike the standard Fender scale of twenty-five-and-a-half inches). It was a fair strategy – but, again, it didn't work, and the Series 24 models were dropped by 2005.

Tonn also inherited the Showmaster line of superstrats – the renamed Stagemaster line – and this, too, struggled to survive. He puts it simply enough: "At the price they sold for, you were going to buy an Ibanez guitar way before you were going to buy a Showmaster."[83] About all he could do to try to increase the visibility of the Showmasters was to offer some bolder finishes. This resulted in models such as the Skull & Crossbones version and the Rally Stripe version (the Rally with a three-tuners-a-side headstock rather than the line's regulation reverse headstock), both of which were introduced to a short life during 2003.

It was around this time that a new policy by Fender took some of the strain from Squier (and also Fender) when it came to competing with other brands. Bill Mendello, who was by now president of Fender, explains what happened. "The original decision to create the Squier brand, back in the early 80s, was simply: how do we compete in the low and mid range," he says. "We decided then that we would do it with Squier. Later, we had to decide how to compete with the Ibanezes of the world, how to compete in the heavy metal market, how to compete with the strange shapes. And we tried Squier. And it didn't work." So Fender changed tack … and went out to buy other guitar companies.

An early success had come with Fender's acquisition of Guild, back in 1995, then Jackson/Charvel, in 2002, and then a licensing deal with Gretsch a year or so later. "Obviously, when you decide to become acquisitive, you don't just go off and acquire the company you want the same day," Mendello says. "You have to wait for the right company to become available – and a couple of years after we considered this, for example, Jackson became available. We said here's a great opportunity."[84]

The purchase – which included the acquisition of Jackson and Charvel's inventory, trademarks, and designs from Akai along with a Jackson/Charvel factory in California – was of great significance, because it removed the necessity for Squier (and Fender) to continue to make superstrat-like guitars – guitars that nobody seemed much interested in when they had Squier (or Fender) on the head. Now Fender, corporately, could sell Jackson and Charvel superstrats, which certainly were in demand.

Meanwhile, Squier's Showmaster line shuffled on for a few years, and it provided the home for an early signature-edition Squier. Fender had kicked off its own take on the signature or artist guitar – a bespoke instrument modelled on the tastes of a famous player – with the Fender-brand Eric Clapton and Yngwie Malmsteen Stratocasters, back in 1988. For Squier, the 2003 Jason Ellis Showmaster did not, however, follow the same idea of emulating the nuances of a god-like player's guitar and placing the result before his adoring fans. Squier had discovered lifestyle.

Since the mid 90s, it was becoming apparent to Squier's various brand managers that there was a youthful movement taking shape which centred on 'new' sports such as skateboarding and BMX biking – and many of the kids who took part played in bands, too. They were not likely to be interested in an Eric Clapton Stratocaster.

Alex Perez, who began working at Fender in 1990 and moved to artist relations three years later, says it made sense to follow the scene and to get involved. Squier's catalogues and ads had begun to reflect skateboarding themes, starting in 1989 with a skateboarder amid graffiti on the cover of that year's catalogue, and then in 1997 with another skateboarder (apparently balancing on a table-top while clutching a Pro Tone Strat) who was used on a slew of promo material. A further ad from that period showed pro skateboarder Remy Stratton performing what aficionados would recognise as a frontside pop shove-it … while hanging on tight to his Affinity Strat, and all in the cause of

★★★ SERIES 24 ★★★★★★★

Wanna step into a meaty, beefy tone that packs a punch and lets everyone know you mean business? Then strap on any one of our Series 24 guitars. The Series 24 set-neck guitars are all about bang for your hard-earned buck and offer Duncan Designed humbucking pickups loaded into solid-body, semi-hollow and hollow-body models. The shorter 24-3/4" scale length—hence the name Series 24—has a different feel and allows greater playability up and down the neck.

The M-50 features two humbucking pickups that pack a hefty punch, plus the jumbo nickel silver frets and dot inlays make it a breeze to play. Want a guitar that'll set you apart from the pack? Well, this is the real deal!

M-50
034-5000
CRIMSON TRANSPARENT RED (15)

M-70
034-7000
MOON BLUE (96)

The M-70 is equipped with all the essential tools you'll need to rock the house! Featuring a single cutaway, set-neck body, jumbo frets and dot inlays, the M-70's got Duncan Designed humbucking pickups onboard for maximum crunch.

All set-neck Series 24 guitars feature Duncan Designed humbucking pickups

BLACK METALLIC (65)

If you're a player seeking a traditional-style instrument with Duncan Designed pickups that looks, sounds, and plays like a guitar twice the price, search no further! The M-77 sounds amazing! Featuring a single cut-away body with set-in Mahogany neck and Rosewood fingerboard, carved Maple top, and multi-lam Black/Ivory binding, this beauty has a snappy sound and a definitive tone all its own.

M-77
034-7700
CHERRY SUNBURST (30)

Squier by Fender

2003 Showmaster H Cat Guitar SLE Black

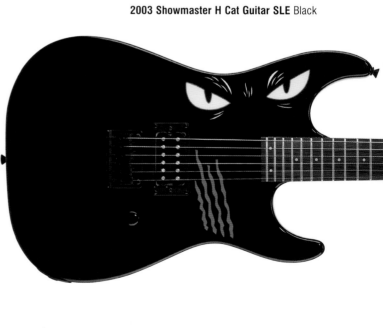

SQUIER ELECTRICS

2002 S-73 Black

■ Fender had bought **DeArmond** in 1997 and began a new line of guitars with the brand (ad, *above*), using designs from **Guild**, another Fender 90s acquisition. When the DeArmonds failed, some were converted into the Squier **Series 24**, starting in 2002 and including the S-73 (*above*) and various M models (catalogue page, *opposite*). Squier occasionally offered **limited editions**, such as this Showmaster H Cat Guitar (*left*) complete with scratch and eyes. **Skateboarding** was never far away, with an Affinity Strat aloft in this **1999 catalogue** (*above*).

promoting the latest incarnation of the Strat Pak. For guitarists of a certain vintage, that ad might have recalled the series of classic 50s and 60s Fender ads, headlined 'You Won't Part With Yours Either', which featured guitars in unlikely outdoor action settings.

The X-Games began in 1995 and soon became a big annual action-sports festival. It provided another focus for Fender to go and meet young music-minded athletes. At the X-Games – and other similar events – Fender would offer guitars as trophies and take the opportunity to mix with a new type of customer. "A lot of these kids have an interest in music and think it's cool," Perez says, "but they never really get to put their hands on a guitar until someone shows them one. It's not like they would be going along to a music store and checking it out – that would be too uncool. So now we had ways to bring the guitars to them."

Perez also witnessed Fender teaming up with new-sports company K2 in the late 90s. "One of the things we did with them was the Roadhouse," Perez explains, "which was basically a travelling Fender display. K2 had the model already: they were using these special vehicles to stage demos for their inline skates, showing up to, say, a sports chalet so that people could come and try out their stuff. We got about four of them. You could open up the doors of the trailer, and there'd be guitars hanging on the walls, amps set up with little headphone stations, and you could try stuff out."[85]

Simplicity and accessibility seemed to be the rationale behind the Fender-brand Tom DeLonge Stratocaster, launched in 2001 to match the guitar that DeLonge used regularly with his band, blink-182. This Fender model had a single humbucker and just one control knob – for volume, of course. Admirably, DeLonge just wanted to plug straight in and play. The year after the Fender appeared, Squier, too, issued a DeLonge guitar – with a similar set of simple specs – and it marked the brand's first signature model.

When Mike Tonn was still at Musician's Friend, before he moved to Fender, Richard McDonald showed him a prototype of the Fender DeLonge at the Winter 2000 NAMM trade show. McDonald steered and directed Squier to a lot of these new possibilities. "I kind of knew who blink-182 were, but not really Tom DeLonge," Tonn says. "I knew Richard, though, and put my faith in his conviction that this Fender model would do well if I picked it up for our catalogue. He agreed to give it to Musician's Friend and add black as an exclusive colour for us. He was right – and we sold thousands of these guitars. When I became the Squier guy, I spoke to Tom DeLonge, told him this story, and asked him if we could do a Squier version of the same Fender model. He thought it would be a great idea."[86]

McDonald adds that younger players like DeLonge immediately understood the attraction of a Squier model in a way that the older generation of guitar stars probably would not or could nor grasp. "It was real logical to say to guys like Tom DeLonge, look, your customers don't have $800, but we can give them a really cool guitar for less," McDonald says. "And they see that. They have a completely different mindset. There's no ego attached – and these are smart marketers. They understand the advertising and marketing world that they grew up in. They understand how it works, that it's all about community and engagement."[87]

Take Jason Ellis, for example. Ellis is an Australian who moved to the USA in his teens and became a successful skateboarder and martial artist, among quite a few other things. He played in a band, too, and Alex Perez says the idea of a Squier signature model made perfect sense to Ellis. "He was saying hey, do you think it would be cool if we made this my model? And we said yes, that's totally possible. He was blown away, and he was asking what we had to do to make it happen. Next thing you know, we're making a model. Everything aligned. Seemed like the timing was right. After he stopped riding and was slowing down – I guess it takes a toll on your body and he needed to take a break – next thing you know he becomes the guy on the microphone and he's on TV all the time, interviewing athletes and bands. It was a perfect fit."

The Squier Jason Ellis Signature Showmaster was essentially a Showmaster HH – the 24-fret model with two humbuckers, locking nut and vibrato, and the usual reverse headstock – but with Ellis's Red Dragon logo on the front of the body and a single-coil instead of a humbucker in the neck position. The logo comes from one of the dragon tiles in the game Mahjong and means 'balance' – which, rather appropriately, was adopted by an elite team of skaters, including Ellis, who then also used it for their RDS Skate Supply business. "With that guitar, we were reaching a different set of kids," Perez says. "Again, these were kids who wouldn't walk into a Guitar Center … but they would walk into a skate shop – and they're seeing a guitar hanging on the wall, with that cool logo on it that they know. It was attainable and it was affordable. That was the beauty of it."[88]

A further Showmaster signature guitar issued in 2003 was the Jimmy Shine model. Mike Tonn says it reveals another aspect of Squier's different approach to signature tie-ins, without the traditional attachment of a guitar god. In this case, Squier opted for a custom motorcycle-maker. "The So-Cal speed shop has worked with Fender for years," Tonn says. "Cars and bikes and guitars have always gone together. Jimmy Shine is a Southern California custom bike-maker – and I liked his artwork and his style. We got in touch and we started talking about Squier. It was a little easier to grab folks that are not gigantic at the time and migrate them into Squier. If they're smart marketing people, which typically they are, they don't care that it's not a Fender – they see the marketing advantages of getting their names out there."

Tonn says Jimmy Shine did a great job at the launch of the guitar at the NAMM show, with the very visible attraction of a fabulous bike on the stand. It was another step to open up Squier to a wider audience, to reach beyond conventional guitar marketing. "I think that was the start of something for Squier," he suggests. "Prior to that, there was hardly any marketing to speak of for the brand. It was a good move at the time: it gave some visibility to Showmaster, and in the big picture it helped Squier."[89]

2002 Tom DeLonge Stratocaster Polar White

2002 Showmaster HS Jason Ellis Signature
Black Metallic

2003 Showmaster H Jimmy Shine SLE Black

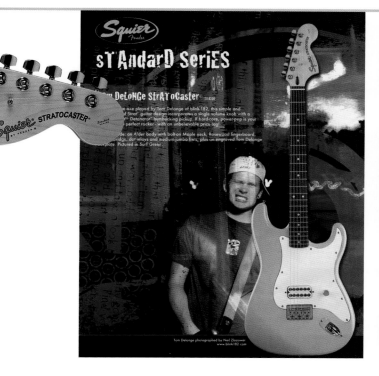

Squier Fender
sTAndarD SeriES
m DeLoNGe StrAToCaster

Tom Delonge photographed by Neil Zlozower
www.blink182.com

■ Squier reached out to new players with the mobile **Roadhouse** (*below*) at sports events. **Jason Ellis** (catalogue page, *right*) was typical of the new role models – he was a martial artist, skateboarder, and quite a lot more. His Squier model (main guitar) first appeared in 2002. Another featured artist was **Jimmy Shine**, a motorcycle maker (guitar *opposite, bottom*). Guitar players were not ignored, however: **Tom DeLonge** of blink-182 had a simple signature model (*top*). Custom features like matching head colours (*top*) were on some **FSR** models (Factory Special Run).

Jason Ellis Showmaster 133 3000

In the market for a cool 'n' unique guitar? This Squier® Showmaster™ guitar is inspired by celebrated skateboarder and guitarist, Jason Ellis, and features a 24 fret neck, reverse headstock, and boasts the same sleek body design that the Showmaster™ Series models are famous for. This guitar comes equipped with a Duncan-Design® Detonator™ humbucking pickup in the bridge position and a single-coil neck position pickup. It also has Jason's specially designed graphic logo on the body signifying 'balance.' Also featuring a solid Basswood body with a bolt-on Maple neck and Rosewood fingerboard, dot inlays, and medium jumbo frets. Available in Black Metallic and Metallic Red.

Jason Ellis photographed by Frank Barbara.

In February 2003, the Squier pricelist showed an Indonesian Bullet ($165.99), a Chinese or Indonesian Mini ($165.99), two Chinese Affinity Strats and a Chinese Affinity Tele ($248.99–$282.99), a Chinese Tom DeLonge Strat ($299.99), seven Korean or Indonesian Series 24 models ($308.99–$1126.99), three Indonesian Standard Strats and two Indonesian Standard Teles ($332.99–$382.99), a Chinese Jagmaster ($415.99), a Chinese Showmaster Jason Ellis model ($448.99), and a Chinese Showmaster model ($499.99). There were also six limited edition models "available for a limited time only": an Indonesian Bullet Special in Orange ($165.99); a Chinese Affinity Strat in Aztec Gold ($248.99); an Indonesian Standard Strat in four custom finishes and pickguard styles ($332.99); a Chinese Showmaster HH Holoflake – Holoflake being an unusual sort of reflective speckled blue-green-pink ($382.99); a Chinese Showmaster HH in Graffiti Yellow ($448.99); and a Chinese Showmaster Jimmy Shine model ($499.99). (Note that, as with all the pricelists quoted throughout this book, these are the full list prices; real-life street prices are almost always lower.)

The Mini was a scaled-down Strat-like Squier, introduced in 1999 and intended to fit younger hands, and the Jagmaster, the modified Jazzmaster design from the obsolete Vista Series of the 90s, was first reissued in 2000. The limited editions were a result of Mike Tonn's intention to provide a wider set of colour options for Squier models, the better to compete with what other makers offered at the time. "I would send out paint and graphics samples to Yako in China and others and say, Can you paint this? We would go back and forth to get it right," he recalls. "I was trying to target different consumers with these extra colours. When I added Candy Apple Red or Shoreline Gold, I thought maybe a more traditional player would gravitate toward that. Black Metallic? We knew the heavy-metal guy would look at that, especially when it comes to the Standard Double Fat Strat. And something like Sherwood Green, well, that seemed to be in the middle somewhere."

Tonn saw a steady development in the abilities of the various factories that Squier used during his brief but active period running the brand in the early 2000s. "They were just getting up to speed to build good guitars," he says. "That process has evolved over time to where they make awesome guitars today. Back then, they were in a transitional period. The Indonesian Cort factory was really state-of-the-art. They made better guitars than the Chinese factories, although the Yako factory was by far the best there. Fujigen in Japan was the overall best factory, but I couldn't afford to have Squier guitars made there." Tonn recalls his tenure at Squier fondly, and considers it the beginning of a new era. "It started to define Squier as not just a me-too brand. Squier became more: hey, this is what we are, this is what we're about."[90]

Squier marked its 20th anniversary in 2002 with the presence of a commemorative neckplate on most of that year's models. The neckplate had this inscription: "20th Anniversary Squier By Fender: Freedom Of Expression Since 1982." Richard McDonald saw it as a further affirmation of Squier's growing importance within the Fender operation. "We'd already realised that Fender's little brother was in high school," McDonald says, "and then it was oh no, he's not in high school, he's just graduated – he's 20 years old! But he's worth 60 million dollars. So I started treating Squier exactly like I'd treat Fender, which was to celebrate anniversaries, to celebrate artists, to pay homage to Fender's history."[91]

Justin Norvell had started at Fender back in 1995, working briefly in a number of posts until he went to product development a year later. At the end of 2002, he began a new job running Squier, replacing Mike Tonn, who became marketing manager for the Fender brand. Norvell did the same as every new arrival in the Squier hot-seat: he took a long hard look at the landscape. Behind him, he saw a brand that had changed identity every couple of years or so and had no evident long-term plan in place. "If four people in a row have the job for two years each, that's probably not good," he says. "At one point, it was all seven-strings and detuned guitars and sparkle finishes, then it went super-traditional and was just a very normal product offering, and then it was kind of scattered with a bunch of different models."

Immediately in front of Norvell was the charge to try to refocus Squier to something simpler, to offer a clear set of good–better–best models that were easy to tell apart. To that end, he made sure the three Squier series were well defined: Bullet, Affinity, and Standard, in that order: good, better, best. "The Bullet had no tremolo and one pickup; the next one, Affinity, had the thinner body and some basic colour choices; and then the next version up, the Standard, had the better two-point tremolo assembly and more options, alnico pickups, full-thickness body, and so on."

One style of model that Norvell added to the line proved to be particularly long-lasting, the Black & Chrome Strat and Tele. He describes these dark and shiny creatures as an attempt to add a little more edge to the regular Squier Standard series. "Younger players mostly play aggressive music. There's always your young blues phenoms, yet at the same time, unscientifically, I'd say 70 or 80 percent of people that start playing guitar start playing pretty heavy music. And OK, over time a lot of those get more musical and maybe mellow out. But these guitars were for the heavy guys." The Black & Chrome models were a way to keep the Strat and Tele designs intact, without messing with the specs but still providing that modern, edgy, sleek appeal.

"I'd seen chrome pickguards and mirrored stuff over time," Norvell says, "but we also gave them dark rosewood fretboards, black bodies, painted black headstocks, chrome knobs, black pickups. I remember I had a keyring with all these different pickguard materials on it, a hundred different types of plastics and stuff. I'd just go through them. The mirrored material was on there, and it was appealing. On the sample we got, the mirrored material was on top of the plastic, and you could scratch it off, so we had them go back and reinvent it so that it's clear plastic with the mirrored

2003 Showmaster HH Holoflake SLE Holoflake

2004 M-77 Gold Top LE Frost Gold

■ A number of Squier models were fading from popularity, including the superstrat-like **Showmasters** (such as this unusual Holoflake-finish example, *above*) and the Guild-like **Series 24** (such as this limited edition M-77 with gold finish, *right*). A successful new addition was a line of **Black & Chrome** finish models (see Strat, *top*, and ad, *opposite*), launched in 2004. A couple of years earlier, Squier quietly celebrated its **20th anniversary** with a special neckplate on 2002's guitars, as well as some print ads (*opposite*).

HAPPY BIRTHDAY DEAR SQUIER

2005 Black & Chrome Standard Stratocaster Gloss Black

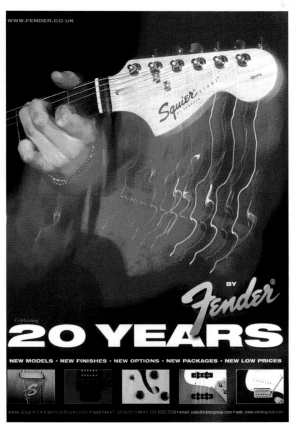

SQUIER ELECTRICS

83

material on the bottom. Right, I said, we'll have that." The Black & Chrome Strat and Tele joined the line in 2004, with a Fat Strat the following year, and at the time of writing they're still there and they're still popular.

With the basic series clarified, Norvell developed the new 'lifestyle' element that had become important to marketing the brand. "In a lot of international markets, Squier is more of a budget Fender for players across all ages, whereas in North America it's much more youth-oriented," he says. "At that age, if someone gets into skateboarding or playing football, that becomes an identity, an aesthetic that you can ascribe to. If there's something to ascribe to, it's more likely to help someone stick with playing and really get into being a musician, because that's an age where people experiment. Do I want to play guitar? Well, maybe not; maybe I want to be an athlete."

Norvell says Fender continued to find that a lot of extreme-athletes also liked to play loud rock and punk, exemplified by the bands who would perform at X Games and similar events. Fender was by now a sponsor of the X Games and took advantage of the easy affinity between athletes and guitarists. "It spoke to that whole youth culture – skateboard, surfboard, punk rock – and it all fell together very naturally," he recalls. "We didn't have some initiative or meeting where we decided to go after this or do that. It happened naturally through bands and events. Like when someone said hey, you should meet our friend Mike Vallely, he's a pro skater, he's in a band that he fronts, and he plays guitar. All of a sudden you realised there were four other pro skaters who play guitar, and their events showed how rock music was hewn into the event and the lifestyle. It was and still is a pretty good fit for that specific set of people."[92]

Vallely summed it up. "Whether I'm writing poems or songs, playing my guitar, or riding my skateboard, for me it's all about self-expression," he said. "Being creative and having fun doesn't require talent and there are no rules. It's all about being an individual, doing your own thing, getting it out there, and putting it down. The creative pursuit is its own destination and its own reward. It's what makes our lives interesting and colorful. There's hope and faith in music, painting, skateboarding … in doing your own thing, whatever it is. I believe that through art we can change the world. Sometimes it's as simple as picking up a guitar."[93]

One of the most important innovations during Norvell's years at Squier was the introduction of the Vintage Modified series. Fender's classic designs, the Telecaster and the Stratocaster, have always been easy to chop about to suit the way individual players want them to be. Guitarists and repairers have always hacked out pickups, thrown in humbuckers, rewired stuff, bolted on different necks – any number of possibilities, thanks in some measure to those super-adaptable original designs. "And there's another part to this," Norvell says. "I'll admit I spend a lot of time poring over websites, history, archives, books … and you soon get to the pages for the Bronco or the Starcaster or the Maverick or the Custom – all that weird Fender stuff and the esoteric ephemera. That all captivates me. It speaks to the modular nature of the guitars, which is so unique compared to a lot of other manufacturers."

Norvell has always been attracted to this adaptable culture at the heart of Fender design. It's what prompted new pickguard templates for Squier models, starting early in 2004 and designed, as the press release described it, "to follow those found on Fender guitars, so that it is easier for musicians to customize their instrument with different pickguards and pickups".

He traces the trend back to the grunge guitarists of the early 90s, who popularised the idea of buy-it-cheap and bend-it-to-your-will. "So much of that was fuelled by the pawn-shop find," he says, "by people playing Mosrites and Univoxes and modified Mustangs and Musicmasters. You'd never even seen some of these guitars that all of a sudden were being played on a global stage. And for a while now since that grunge debut, this is the type of guitar that has held a place for guitar players under thirty. It tied in perfectly with how we wanted the Squier line to be more youth-oriented and more fun."[94]

Vintage Modified is not one of those Squier series names that appears on the guitars themselves – like Standard or Affinity, for example – but is more a way to group similar models together in catalogues and pricelists. It first turned up to define models like the Tele Custom, launched in 2003, and the Tele Custom II, the following year. Both these ideas had been started in Mike Tonn's time. They merged features of the 70s Fender Tele Custom and Deluxe models, with a pair of humbuckers on the Custom and P-90s on the Custom II. The Squier guys probably thought things couldn't get much hipper than a humbucker'd Tele. And then along came the '51.

The July 2004 press release that announced the new model was innocuous enough. "Squier expands its Vintage Modified series of guitars with the introduction of the new Jagmaster II and Squier '51 guitars at this summer's NAMM show. The Vintage Modified Series is comprised of guitars that feature modern twists on classic designs, built with popular modifications from the get-go." The updated Jagmaster was the second reissue of the 90s Vista Series model (the "II" suffix wasn't ultimately used). The release continued: "The all new Squier '51 is a value-priced instrument offering unique looks and functionality. This guitar is a melting pot of vintage and modern, combining '51 P Bass cosmetics, a Stratocaster guitar body shape, and a tinted Telecaster guitar neck. Its clean appearance belies its true nature, with tonal possibilities galore via the instrument's rotary selector and push-pull coil tap. US MSRP is $248.99."

The origins of the '51 lie in that partiality of Norvell's for sifting through history books to look for inspiration, for "things from the past that never were but could have been" as he describes it. "At one point, I had open a big spread of a 1951 P Bass," he recalls, "and I just looked at it and thought, what if it were a guitar?"[95] That was the first year for the Precision Bass, or P Bass as it's often called. Fender's revolutionary electric bass guitar was the first of its kind anywhere in the world to be sold commercially. For once, the well-worn

2003 California Series Stratocaster Walnut

2004 Vintage Modified Telecaster Custom II Vintage Blonde

2003 X-155 White Heat SE Cobalt Blue Metallic

■ **Vintage Modified** was a new Squier series launched in 2004. This Tele Custom II (main guitar) is 'vintage' in that it's based on a Tele Custom, 'modified' in that it has revised pickups and hardware. **California** models (Strat, *top*) were made in China and sold only in that country, starting in 2003. A few late models crept out from **Series 24** (special edition X-155, *above*) and **Showmaster** (ad with **Andreas Kisser** of Sepultura, *top*). And let's not forget skateboarding: **Mike Vallely** (ad, *opposite*) was a revered pro skater with a band and a guitar.

phrase is accurate: it changed the sound of pop music. You probably know how it looked: a double-cut body shape that foreshadowed the Strat, finished in see-through blonde; a curved Tele-like two-knob metal control panel; a big black pickguard; one pickup in the middle; and a long maple neck with a Tele-style headstock shape.

Norvell got to work with his colleagues around the start of 2004 to see if a P Bass could indeed be turned into a guitar. Clay Lyons was among those who worked with him to realign history. Lyons had joined Fender two years earlier and was a graphic designer for the company. "We're staring at a picture of a '51 P Bass and a Squier Strat," Lyons recalls, "and then we started to frankenstein the thing up, morphing the two together, switching out different necks, headstocks, and pickguard configurations. That was my role back then: we'd come up with concepts and create dozens of mock-ups in Photoshop, different variations, and present them to the product manager."[96]

The mock-ups started with everything more or less the same as a '51 Precision, but with a lone Tele-bridge-like single-coil pickup located in the P Bass position, plus some contouring to the body and a two-tone sunburst finish, which made it more like a Strat or the second ('54) incarnation of the Precision. Norvell took one of the Photoshop mock-ups out to the Cort factory in Indonesia and talked through some choices of hardware. "Two weeks later I had the first prototype … and we were a little underwhelmed," he recalls. "I imagined it would be more than it was when it was finally in my hands."

Next, they decided to take things in what Norvell calls a more modern direction. First they removed the mid-body single-coil and instead decided on a ceramic humbucker at the bridge. They fiddled around with more mock-ups in Photoshop, trying the new humbucker'd body with a rosewood-board Strat neck or a Tele-like maple neck. "We liked that look, with the Tele neck – and the prototype, which arrived about three weeks after the first one, sounded great," he says. "But I still felt it needed more, feature-wise, although we didn't want to alter the aesthetic. So we added a colour-matched neck single-coil to blend into the pickguard, preserving the look."

When they added the slanted alnico single-coil at the neck, the simple two-knob volume-and-tone of the earlier versions was no longer appropriate. But it felt wrong to add a switch to what was always intended to be a simple P-Bass-inspired guitar. "So we removed the tone knob in favour of a rotary selector," Norvell says, "which, of course, is very un-Fender. But again, that kept the clean, vintage look intact."

It was all coming together now. They knew they were on to something, and the factory in Indonesia was in its stride. "Cort was a place we knew could make good stuff," Norvell says. "They'd used these pickups in the Squier Tele Special, and of course they had plenty of Strat bodies and Tele necks." The final sonic twist was to give the volume control a push/pull coil-split. "That added a bunch of tonal options and functionality, but without altering the look very much at all. It wouldn't have been right with more knobs and switches or overt extra pickups. In the end, it was quite a pleasing balance between usefulness, being different, and looking great. Modern, but with a classic appeal. And all for the price of a nice effects pedal."

A final look was established: blonde, black, or two-tone sunburst finish, with a white or black pickguard on the blonde one and a white guard only for the other two. The white guard had a white-cover single-coil, the black guard a black one, and the humbucker was always black. "That gave it a two-tone vibe that is kind of cool," Norvell says.[97] The three-position rotary control offered neck, both, or bridge pickup, and with it set in the both or bridge position, the push/pull on the volume knob could split the bridge humbucker to single-coil. It's simpler and more intuitive than that sounds, and it provided a very effective tonal array.

This was the Squier Vintage Modified approach in a heightened state. As Clay Lyons puts it: "Squier is a brand that we can take chances with, mess with a little bit, and that doesn't upset the consumer. In fact, they kind of expect that from the brand. Whereas with Fender, you don't have the ability to take chances like that. With Fender, if you move a screw a millimetre to the left, you get hate mail."[98]

But what about that model name? It didn't even appear on the headstock, which said just "Squier By Fender". The hate-mail brigade would surely argue that it should have been called the '54, what with its contoured body that didn't appear on the P Bass until that year. "We weren't being too precious with history," Norvell smiles, "and we used that name simply because the inspiration came from the '51 P Bass. It was a working title that kind of went out the door that way. It got to the point where we were getting ready to release it, and everybody inside had already been calling it that. So '51 it was."

Despite the changes along the way, the '51 took just six months from idea to production, with the original inspiration more or less intact. "People have said to me, well, this guitar is part '51 P Bass, part Strat, because of the body, and part Telecaster, because of the headstock. But in all honesty, if anything it's 80 percent '51 P Bass. So much more of the design comes from that, and it's a lot less of a hybrid than sometimes people think it is."[99]

The new model got its release at the 2004 summer NAMM show, and then it went out to the stores – and it was an instant hit. "The Squier '51 is a hot-rod in the truest sense of the word, [and it delivers] a broad spectrum of tones," wrote *Guitar Player* magazine. "This is a fun guitar to play, and with its custom look, hip tones, and downright amazing price, the Squier '51 easily nabs an Editors' Pick Award."[100] With a street price most often well below its $250 list, this excellent Indonesian axe seemed suddenly to be everywhere. It became an impulse buy for guitarists at all levels and a test-bed favourite. "It was the first time that Squier had a buzz on it about something," Norvell says. "It had mass appeal, and not only for beginners, because it also had that funky pawn-shop attraction to a wider range of players, the way that Danelectros had when they came back out a few years ago."[101] There was also the internet. "I had no idea

2005 '51 Vintage Blonde

2004 '51 Vintage Blonde

2004 '51 2-Tone Sunburst

2004 '51 Black

90

SQUIER ELECTRICS

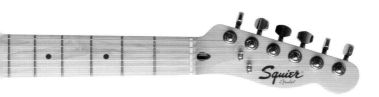

■ The Squier '51, new in 2005, was a sensation. **Justin Norvell** (*below*) wanted a guitar based on a '51 Precision Bass, and is pictured considering the options (*inset* are two early **mock-ups**). The result was a guitar cheap enough and modular enough to satisfy a craze for modifying and adapting the wildly popular '51. It's pictured here in its four regular stock forms: **blonde** with black or white pickguard; **sunburst** with white pickguard; and **black** with white pickguard.

the '51 would be as big as it was," laughs Richard McDonald, who still kept an eye on the Squier line from his vantage point heading the Fender operation. "The online community was already out there," he says, "and the '51 didn't create the community, but it became the flag that they swarmed around. It was the right guitar at the right time – that tipping-point thing. If I could figure out how to do it all the time, I would! You go with your instincts and you try to make a compelling product. But that one was huge. It blew up from the online interest."[102]

Online forums discovered the '51 and made it their own. Andy Zuckerman, or Andy Z as he's known, started the Squier '51 Modders Forum in 2005. These days, Zuckerman is part of the product development team at Line 6, the California-based guitar gear company, but back then he noticed that the '51 had caught on "like wildfire", as he describes it, and he saw a growing number of posts about the guitar on a variety of sites. "I figured, coming from an IT background, that I could post up a sister forum in hours to collect all this great data in one place," Zuckerman recalls. "I posted on all these sites where my site was. And like from the movie line: if you build it, they will come. I tried to build the forum sections simply into what users wanted to see, and not what I wanted. It grew much bigger than I expected – and today the database is busting at the seams."

The word Modders in the name of Zuckerman's forum underlines one of the key attractions of the '51. It was cheap enough to buy and immediately start chopping and 'improving'. He reckons the most common mod among the posters on his site is to replace the bridge, followed by the pickguard, and then the pickups. A popular supplier of the bits to bolt on is Guitarfetish, he says. "Their prices fit the cost justification of this guitar. One of the wildest mods I've seen was where someone made a sitar-based '51, and I guess it must have been their take on the old Coral sitar-guitar. But I think most folks just want to individualise a '51 as an extension of themselves – and being such an inexpensive guitar, they don't feel like they're taking a chance on ruining it. You surely don't see many user-modded Custom Shop guitars."

Zuckerman says he thinks the '51 was suited to modding not only because of its price, but also because its construction makes it straightforward to interchange parts. "I think it really fit Leo's original idea of something easy to repair, modify, and customise," he says. "Sometimes the Squier line offers more real gems. I have an Affinity Tele in Butterscotch Blonde that I have modded to the gills. I'm good friends with guitar legend Albert Lee, and he sits in and jams with me when he's in town. Albert played this guitar and couldn't believe how well it sounded and played, and he was floored when I told him I built it, including the guitar, for less than $250."[103]

Remarkably, the '51 didn't last too long in the line, despite its popularity, and it was removed from the Squier catalogue during 2007 – although not before a short run of Custom Shop versions were made by John Cruz, complete with a Fender brand, a Tele bridge-pickup, and a price tag more than 20 times the Squier original.

Demand for the '51s didn't go away after Squier stopped their production. "Squier '51 mania has officially started," wrote KwadGuy, a poster to retailer Harmony Central's online forum, a while after the model's demise. "We all know the Squier '51s are in hot demand as mod platforms or just as all-around great guitars out of the box. The going price for a decent one seems to be around $200-ish shipped on eBay. However, how about a new one in box? Well, a friend of mine listed one on Craigslist last week for $250/obo. Black, new in unopened box. Three guys contacted him within a couple of hours of the post and got in a bidding war. He sold it for $460 and a box of D'Addario guitar strings – and one of the guys who didn't get it tried to get him to hold off, offering $500-plus."[104]

Norvell recalls that even while the Squier '51 was still being made, he would hear from retailers, consumers, forum posters, and others that they ought to make a regular Fender-brand version. And in 2011, four years after the Squier had stopped, that's what they did. The Pawn Shop Fender '51 was a lot like the Squier – but with a Fender brand, Japanese manufacture, and a $1,099.99 list price. A good number of Fender models have of course been turned into Squiers, right from day one. But this was the first time a Squier model had become a Fender.

In 2004, the same year the '51 appeared, a new slogan was seen attached to Squier publicity. "Stop dreaming, start playing" summed up the brand's new-found confidence. "We wanted to create a phrase that reached people on an emotional level rather than leaving it to specs or features," Norvell says. "And knowing that so many young people imagine themselves as rock stars in their bedrooms in front of the mirror, and that many older beginners would love to play but find it hard, we felt it was a call to action on all of these levels." Also, he sensed there was something in the air. "There was kind of a zeitgeisty wave around this time, when guitar really broke through to the masses. There was the *School Of Rock* movie in 2003. And then when the *Rock Band* and *Guitar Hero* trend hit a few years later, there was a whole new group of people being drawn to try out a real guitar after playing one of those games for a while."

Meanwhile, there was perhaps a little payback from the Custom Shop for borrowing the '51 for that short run, and it arrived in the shape of the Squier Master series. The Korean M-80 and Indonesian M-80 Special, designed by Todd Krause in the Shop, were a development of the Series 24 guitars. They came with twin humbuckers and a set-neck (M-80) or a bolt-on neck (Special). The Korean Chambered Tele HH and Chinese Thinline Tele HH also had a pair of humbuckers and set necks, plus Les Paul-style control layouts. The Korean Esprit was based on a Fender model from 1984 and marked a brief return to Squier matters by Dan Smith, who had designed the Japanese-made original and now provided an 80s prototype to work from. All five Master models were gone from the line within a couple of years.

2005 '51 Black

2004 '51 2-Tone Sunburst

2006 '51 Blue

SQUIER ELECTRICS

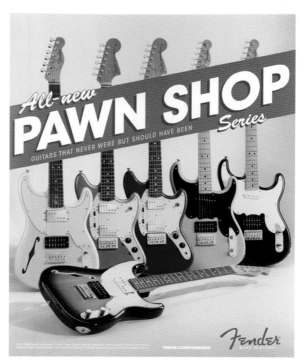

■ The most common **mod** made to the cheap and malleable '51 was to change the bridge. Two examples here show a black one with an added Eyb **sitar bridge** and a sunburst with a retrofit **Bigsby**. Pickups were a common target, too, as was the pickguard. There were custom '51 finishes for Japanese distributor Yamano, such as this blue one (*left*). **Nick Curran**, ex-Fabulous Thunderbirds, plays a nicely personalised '51 (*top*). Strangely, Squier dropped the cool '51 in 2007, only reviving the design four years later for a **Fender** Pawn Shop model (*right*), the first time a Squier became a Fender. Meanwhile, the **M-80** (ad, *above*) drew on the expertise of **Todd Krause** in Fender's Custom Shop.

SQUIER ELECTRICS

Justin Norvell left Squier in 2005 to become senior marketing manager for Fender. "I felt very in touch with what Squier was about," he says of his time running the brand. "The people before me and after me have all worked to steward the legacy, to keep Squier what it is, to inspire people to start playing, and to provide value for people who might find a Fender out of reach."[105]

The new product manager was Chris Gill, who still runs Squier at the time of writing. Gill has worked at Fender since 1992, at first in customer service and sales. He moved to marketing as an assistant to Mike Lewis a few years later, and also worked with the factory to plan schedules. His immediate reaction when he got the Squier job was to wonder how on earth he could make any progress with a brand that had enjoyed increasing sales for some years. "But you know how things go in cycles? Sure enough," he laughs, "right at that time, the low-end guitar market, especially in the States, fell through the floor. So I had a big challenge ahead of me."

Gill thought the budget guitar market was saturated with models from any number of brands, Squier included. Also, unquestionably, there was more competition for the cash that, traditionally, people might spend on musical instruments. It all added up to an unnerving dip in sales. "It took me a good year to figure out where I was and where the brand was," Gill recalls. "In the end, the more I looked around, the more I wanted to get back to the roots of what Squier was originally – those really well-made Japanese Fender models. I decided that would be my direction, to try to continue to elevate the brand and the brand's status and to get away from the idea that it was a commodity low-end product."

He wanted to get across to potential customers that Squier *is* Fender. "The most important thing to me when I look at the headstocks is that they say 'Squier By Fender'. People say oh, Squier: isn't that just one of those copy brands that copies Fender guitars? Well, no, actually – it's owned by Fender, and actually it is Fender. So I wanted to create a different perception in the marketplace. It's not some other guitar brand that Fender bought. It is Fender."[106]

This direct connection to Fender is what Squier has to itself, Gill figured, something that no other mere copy brand has. And in tough times, you go back to the core. It meant sweeping away quite a number of existing models, including the Cyclone, the Esprit, and the two M-80s, all dropped by 2007. Out goes the odd stuff; in comes a shift of focus to quality and to traditional packages. For the most part, anyway. Gill kept the two base series of the line, Affinity and Standard, and later, as we'll see, he revised the Deluxe series (2007) and added the Classic Vibe series (2008). But first there were some decorative diversions.

How do you encourage young women to play guitar? In 2001, the Daisy Rock company, at first in collaboration with Schecter guitars, had offered a commercial solution: you make guitars with a look and design that might attract girls. Fender could hardly have failed to notice Daisy Rock's big success. And then, during 2004, an opportunity presented itself when Sanrio, the company that owns the Hello Kitty trademark, approached Fender to make a one-off guitar for a special event. Hello Kitty is the cult Japanese cartoon-like character whose image has appeared on everything from coin purses to cars … and now also guitars. Richard McDonald, the Fender-brands manager, and Morgan Ringwald, then head of Fender's marketing and communication, decided to call Bill Hensley at Sanrio and suggest a meeting to discuss the scope for a licensing deal between Fender and Hello Kitty. A few meetings later, they agreed a deal where Sanrio would grant a licence for Fender to make Squier guitars featuring Hello Kitty images.

Clay Lyons was a graphic designer at Fender and he helped to develop the designs for the Squier Hello Kitty guitars: a Strat, a Mini, and a bass. "The challenge," Lyons says, "was that we didn't want to dial it in, so to speak – we didn't want to just make a pink Strat and put the logo on it somewhere. We wanted to do something that was unique, and so we put some effort into making it original. That ended up being the Hello Kitty-shaped pickguard. It created some problems in manufacturing, because the pickguard of course holds a lot of the wiring chassis for the pickups and everything – so by changing the shape of that, we had some challenges with the factory in getting it right."

Naturally, Sanrio were particular about how their Hello Kitty logos and images were used, and Lyons and the team went through a number of variations back and forth to get it right. The shape of the pickguard for the Hello Kitty Strat had to follow the outline of the character's head – a rounded base, with offset pointed ears and a bow at the top. Once that had been cleared, it was the colours on the rear of the body that provided the next obstacle. "When you flipped the Strat over," Lyons says, "we wanted a pink for the body and a deeper pink for the script name. We probably had more to-and-fro getting that colour right with Sanrio than the pickguard. And of course we wanted it to be a really solid playing guitar: we didn't want to sacrifice playability for the design."[107]

With everything at last finalised, Squier put the designs into limited production. At first, in late 2005, Fender sold the Squier Hello Kitty guitars exclusively through what it described as "MI industry channels and Sanrio stores in major-market shopping malls". A brief notice in an issue of *Newsweek* at the end of 2005 did no harm when the Hello Kitty guitar starred in the top spot of the magazine's Christmas list of "gifts for the musically obsessed". Above the other contenders, such as iPod Nano armbands, the Hecsan Rollup Piano, and iTunes gift cards, sat the $229 Hello Kitty guitar. "Your young rock star can strum along with that darn cat," *Newsweek* advised. "Available in pink or black."[108]

It also seemed that a certain post-modern irony was at work in some quarters. Or post-punk duality, perhaps. One Squier insider describes the attraction of the catty new guitar as somehow "weird *and* cool, in a twisted way". Squier decided to give away some

2006 Hello Kitty Strat Pink

■ **Girls and guitars**: why is that still such a relatively rare combination? Squier sought to boost the idea with a line of **Hello Kitty** guitars in 2006 after a deal with Sanrio, which owns the rights to the cute little character (*right*). Pictured here are the full-size Strat (*above*), with **Kitty-shape pickguard**, and the scaled-down Mini (*below*), with its necessarily more restrained decoration. Squier's **ads** (*opposite*) for the Kittys underlined the joys of playing guitar and moving beyond mere dreams. **Slash** didn't have to dream, either: he's pictured (*opposite*) posing with his Kitty backstage at the 2005 **Billboard Music Awards** in Las Vegas.

2006 Hello Kitty Mini Black

SQUIER ELECTRICS

Hello Kitty guitars at the *Billboard* Awards show in Las Vegas in December 2005. "It was the whole VIP gifting thing, backstage, and we had some of the pink guitars," Lyons says. "Everyone wanted them! Among the first to pick one up was Dave Navarro. He took one look at it and says hey, I'm gonna change out this pickup for something hotter and I'm gonna play this thing and piss off my band. It's gonna be awesome!"[109]

Navarro had been a long-time admirer of Hello Kitty, although probably not in the way its creators intended. "The image itself is more of a symbol of darkness to me than anything else," he told a fan site. "It's the same reason why I have a collection of Barbies and I have a ballerina box. I went through a unicorn phase back in the 90s. There's always some little symbol that's supposed to represent life that I have always found is a much darker symbol than coffins and skulls and crosses and bats."[110]

Navarro was not alone: sightings of the Kitty guitars in non-female hands were reported among the discerning musicians in Bloc Party, Green Day … even Slash wanted one, apparently. Squier had a hit on its hands. In January 2006, the Squier Hello Kitty guitars went on general sale. The press release quoted Richard McDonald: "By teaming up with the Hello Kitty brand, we hope to show young women just how much fun playing the guitar can be." There were logo-adorned picks, straps, gig bags, and amps, too. The Strat and the Mini (with a necessarily simpler logo-and-name on the small body front) stayed on the Squier pricelist until 2009.

Another line of rather different decorated Squiers appeared in 2006, this time a new take on the long tradition of guitarists who customise instruments by sticking decals and phrases and pictures and whatnot to a guitar body. Sometimes it's just words, where the message might be whimsical, other times serious, even political. It dates back at least to the 40s, when Woody Guthrie adorned his acoustic guitar with the famous message: "This machine kills fascists." When artist Shepard Fairey was 14, he discovered punk-rock and skateboarding – "they changed my life," he says – and became aware of people like Joe Strummer with his sticker-laden Tele or Mike Ness of Social Distortion and his similarly personalised SG. This all made a great impression on Fairey's later work as a street artist.

Fairey isn't a musician, but he knew people at Fender through mutual friends, and in 2006 the Custom Shop asked him to make some designs for a signed-and-numbered limited edition Strat and Tele in their high-end series of Fender art guitars. "The methods I use, collage and stencilling, work really well for the guitar," Fairey says. "After I did the Custom Shop project, Fender were so pleased with the results, they said well, why don't we see if we can do something like this that's more for mass consumption?"[111]

Richard McDonald encourages this kind of alliance with artists. "I'm always looking for partnerships," he says, "and people started showing me stuff that Shepard Fairey was doing, the Andre The Giant stuff, early on. I thought wow, this is really cool. I'd been working with Crash, who was a subway graffiti artist in New York, and the guy from Dogtown, Wes Humpston. I'm sending them guitars, saying hey, paint 'em! Here: paint skateboards; paint guitars. I still do it. I give them to tattoo artists, anybody. Every year I try to pick a couple – I just did it with a downhill skier name of Mike Tierney, who's also a graffiti paintcan artist."[112]

The idea of a more mass-appeal guitar attracted Fairey, and Fender immediately suggested this could work for a Squier model – which in Fenderland is as far away as it's possible to get from a Custom Shop art guitar. "Squier is a more affordable guitar," Fairey says, "and a lot of people who are learning the guitar might use a Squier. My feeling with my art, if I can, is to inspire people when they're young and optimistic. My feeling was not that this is going to compromise the value of my art. It was that it's going to put my art in the hands of people where it might be a great way to introduce them to my work. And if they look into my work, they'll see all the music references – they'll see the politics of empowerment in my work. It could be as simple as: it's a cool guitar; it could be as complicated as: it's a gateway to a whole way of thinking and doing things."

Fairey liked, too, the task of devising a look for the guitar that felt authentic and not too slick, even though it was mass produced. He drew on his love of Strummer and Ness and many of his other musical heroes who straddle the history of the stickered guitar. "My goal with the graphics I did for the Squiers was for it to feel like it was layered and an organic accumulation, even though in reality it wasn't," he says. "When I first got into skateboarding and punk, the idea of having something that was brand new was really lame. It would make you look like a rookie – it wasn't authentic. I'd get my Converse Chuck Taylors and immediately take newspaper and brush the black newsprint off to scuff them up. I'd draw all my favourite bands' logos on them: the Sex Pistols, Black Flag, everything. I felt that if I were 14 again and getting my first guitar, that's the kind of feel that I would like."

Fairey came up with three different designs for the Squier Obey Graphic series – effectively custom-finished models in the Indonesian-made Standard series – and all in line with his Obey campaign, intended to provoke people to think about the meaning of propaganda. "No matter what the aesthetic manifestations of propaganda end up being," Fairey says, "there will always be propaganda." The 'Collage' design was available on an HSS Strat or a Fat Tele, the 'Dissent' on an HSS Strat only, and the 'Propaganda' on a Fat Tele only, all launched in 2006.

Fairey reckons that working with a guitar body, and specifically the Strat and Tele shapes, forced him to consider the visual boundaries of a design. "By the boundaries, I mean the edge of the picture plane," he explains. "So if I'm designing in a rectangle I make sure it works well in that rectangle. I very rarely float my artwork in the middle of a page. But the guitar came across as contrived when I tried to design it in a way where everything fit perfectly. It didn't feel spontaneous enough. I made several collages by

2006 Obey Graphic Telecaster Propaganda

2006 Obey Graphic Telecaster Collage

2006 Obey Graphic Stratocaster Dissent

102

■ **Shepard Fairey** is an artist best known for making street art (Fairey at work, *above*), but he jumped at the chance to create a Custom Shop guitar for Fender and then a more widely available set of designs for Squier. The **Obey Graphic** series (Japanese ad, *right*) first appeared in 2006 and included three startling designs: **Propaganda** (*top*), **Collage** (*centre*), and **Dissent** (*bottom*). The edition sold out by 2010. Squier occasionally produces guitars with ad **graphics** for commercial clients, including this 2005 **Miller** Icehouse Strat (*left*).

2005 Icehouse Stratocaster

hand, then scanned those collages, moving them around on the guitar bodies. A couple of things I composed more formally, but mostly I tried to let it feel a little bit looser."

Once the run of Obey Squiers stopped in 2010, there were no more, Fairey says. "So anyone who got one has something special – no one else can get it. I didn't really do it for the money, but it ended up being a nice paycheque. I get criticised a lot for any product I do, because my background is street art, and when you're a street artist you're judged a lot more harshly. So most of the things I do like that, I do because I think it's a culturally relevant way to disseminate my work, and not because it generates revenue. My street art costs a lot to make and to put up, and I've always funded my work selling T-shirts or doing commercial projects. I felt like the Squier guitars were a good project, both in working out financially and in engaging an audience that might not already be familiar with my work."[113]

Some changes were evident at Squier as the brand's new manager Chris Gill focussed the line and developed the instruments. In 2006, Mike Lewis moved from his post at the Fender-licensed Gretsch operation to take over management of all the Fender brands. "Each of the brand guys reported to me, including Chris at Squier," Lewis says. "He'd already taken the brand further and made it a sensible range laid out very clearly. Squier now appealed to a broader range of customer. Not only was it perfect for people just starting, but you might have someone in their thirties or forties, say, who loves Fender but just can't afford $800 or $1,000 at the moment. But they can afford $300, so there's something really nice for them at that price. And they feel like they're buying a Fender."[114]

A change that occurred overseas had little effect on the Squier line but nonetheless formalised a shift that had become significant over time. Dan Smith was there at the birth of Fender Japan in 1982, and he'd witnessed firsthand its critical importance as Bill Schultz headed the buyout from CBS a few years later. However, more recently there had been a gradual but inescapable decline in Fender Japan's standing. In 2005, a year or so before Smith retired from Fender following 25 remarkable years with the company, he saw the inevitable halt to Fender Japan in its existing form.

Japan's guitar market had changed as its economy weakened, Smith explains, and the Japanese were no longer immune to the demand for guitars priced below those that their own country's factories could produce. This all coincided with Fender developing the capabilities of its own factories in Corona and Mexico, which allowed it to make a wider range of more instruments at prices equal to and often better than those available from the remaining Japanese manufacturers who supplied Fender-brand instruments. "In addition," says Smith, "less and less of what was being shipped to Europe and our other export customers was being produced in Japan. These changes eventually meant that Fender Japan as it was originally tasked no longer made sense, and that led to it being dissolved."[115]

That dissolution happened in 2005. Bill Mendello had become CEO at Fender that year, and he explains a little more about the changes to Fender Japan. "It had been a struggle from day one with the Japanese as to what product would be developed for the Japanese market," he says. "In fairness, we knew we had to rely on the two major distributors of Japan to determine what their own market wants. But often, they were building models that we were also making and shipping in. We didn't want that – we wanted a strategy where we complemented each other, where the product we were shipping from the US and elsewhere complemented the product that Fender Japan was making for the Japanese market. That was always the real issue with Fender Japan, and it caused a lot of issues and problems."

Mendello says that the relationship with Fender Japan had gone through many versions. "Over the years, we made probably 50 or 60 changes to the original 1982 joint-venture agreement: fine tuning it here; changing the royalty rate there; things like that." Gradually, he says, Fender had switched a lot of Japanese manufacturing to the Dyna Gakki company. "So, in 2005, Fender Japan was dissolved and we created an entity called Dyna Boeki, to replace Fender Japan."[116] The Japanese distributors remained, with the instruments made in Japan distributed by Kanda Shokai, and the Fender and Squier catalogue, made in the USA and elsewhere, distributed by Yamano.

All of this hardly affected Squier, but it did mark the end of a very important constituent of its history. Meanwhile, in 2007, Squier went back to India – having abandoned production there around 1988 following quality problems – for a new Vintage Modified Strat and Strat HSS and a Tele SH and SSH. Clearly, those earlier problems were long gone. Otherwise, Squier production remained in Indonesia and China.

Chris Gill made other changes here and there. The all-you-need-to-start-playing Paks, first introduced back in the mid 90s as a box with budget guitar, amp, picks, strings, and so on, shifted in 2007 to the new tagline Stop Dreaming, Start Playing! Guitar & Amp Sets (made in China and Indonesia and with list prices between $349.99 and $599.99). The various 'Fat' model names for humbucker'd guitars were replaced around 2007 with HS-style names – H for humbucker, S for single-coil, in various combinations. An HSS model, for example, has a layout of humbucker/single-coil/single-coil (bridge to neck). Also in 2007, the last of the seven-string Squiers was dropped from the line.

The Deluxe series, begun in the early 2000s, was simplified in 2007 to a made-in-Indonesia Strat and Hot Rails Strat (with twin-blade pickups), and the new series was positioned above the Squier Standards in quality and appointments. More interesting was the Classic Vibe series. As we've seen, Gill swept away what he describes as Squier's existing non-traditional models, and now he replaced them with a return to the roots. The plan, he says, was to have the new guitars ready in time to coincide with Squier's 25th anniversary, in 2007. "But various factors with the product development process delayed the launch, which took place the following year," says Gill. Squier's press release

■ New models continued to appear in the **Vintage Modified** series. Some mods were little more than decent tuners on a vintage-looking guitar, exemplified by this attractive Strat (*below*). More often there was a pickup configuration not seen on any vintage model, like the SH Tele (*opposite*), SH meaning single-coil plus humbucker. Squier's **ads** for the series (*above*) emphasised both the look and the specs. If that series was all about getting the balance right, the simpler **Pak** idea continued (the Strat version from 2007, pictured *right*), offering a beginner's box with "everything you need to get started". The guitar was Squier's base **Affinity** model, shown (*right*) in HSS style in an artfully posed **catalogue** shot from 2008.

2007 Vintage Modified Strat
Metallic Red

106

MODIFYING THE VINTAGE

2007 Vintage Modified Tele SH Black

SQUIER ELECTRICS

107

underlined the link back to the most celebrated models in the brand's history. "In 1982, the very first Squier By Fender guitars and basses came from Asia and were prized for their excellent vintage-quality look, feel, sound, and construction," it began. "Those early Squier instruments and their Fender-branded counterparts are now highly sought-after collector's items revered by guitar enthusiasts as models of 'getting it right' while aiming at value-conscious players." The new Classic Vibe Series, claimed the release, mirrored Fender classics but did not bother too much with era-precise or vintage-correct details. Rather, the seven new Chinese-made models were meant to "impart the vibe of classic Fender designs". These first models in the series consisted of 50s and 60s-style Strats, a 50s Tele, and a 50s Duo-Sonic, and they were widely praised.

"The 50s Telecaster was originally sampled for me with an ash body," Gill recalls, "as you would expect for such a guitar. Unfortunately, the cost of ash these days is too expensive for a Squier price-point, so I had to ask the vendor what else could we do to get a good-looking Vintage Blonde colouration." For reference and inspiration, Gill was looking at a particular guitar owned by country artist Vince Gill (no relation). "When they came up with a pine wood option, I knew before I even saw the sample that this could be interesting, as some of the early Teles had been made in pine. The sample body clinched the deal – it looks great! More recently, we added the Butterscotch Blonde colour, and that's very attractive, too."

A couple of new Squier signature models appeared in 2007, and Alex Perez in Fender's artist relations department takes up the story of the first one. "When Deryck Whibley in Sum 41 started playing his Fender Classic Series 72 Telecaster Deluxe, he wanted me to modify it." Perez put in a single Seymour Duncan humbucker for Whibley, replacing the regular pair of Fender Wide Range buckers. "I had to modify the existing pickguard," Perez says, "because in typical fashion he needed it inside a week."

Whibley also wanted the jack shifted from the side of the body to the face. "So I said no problem: I'll just use one of the tone holes or whatever and put the jack there," Perez says. "So I covered up the other control holes – the regular pickguard has four holes, for two volumes and two tones – with little Xs of electrical tape. I guess after he got the guitar, he liked that. Then he ended up putting some red duct tape or something over the three-way switch, the toggle hole – and it became a look, you know?"

The red Xs lent Whibley's Tele a distinctive style that appealed to him. "People started seeing the guitar," Perez says, "and Deryck would email me saying hey, kids are asking me about my guitar after the shows, what do you think? So I said OK, let me to talk to some people here about a signature model. I made him a couple of guitars in Corona that looked like the signature model, and I think one of those is still his backup. But his main guitar remains the original Mexican Fender 72 Deluxe reissue that we modified."

Whibley was pleased with the idea to make his signature model a Squier. It had a single hum, two red Xs on the black body, and a permanent set-up of two control knobs.

"Deryck's whole thing was: if I'm going to have a signature model, I want my fans to be able to afford it," Perez explains. "It was all about the price-point and his fans being able to obtain a guitar, as opposed to them having exactly what he has. It's refreshing when artists have that kind of feeling."[117]

The second of the new-for-2007 signature Squiers was a model for Avril Lavigne, and for that story we need to turn to Billy Siegle. He started at Fender in 1997 – having worked as a guitar tech, engineer, and producer – and quickly moved from marketing to artist relations. "We don't need help designing Telecaster or Stratocaster guitars," Siegle says. "We figured that out long ago. What we do need is marketing partnerships. We're fans of these artists, and they're fans of our body of work. So the question is: how can we work together to give that third point of triangle ownership?"

When the other party is someone like Lavigne, you look at what she's known for, Siegle says. "And while she's not known for being a guitar player, she is known for being very inspirational and having a core audience of a specific demographic of people who look up to her." He means she appeals to young women. And as we saw earlier with the Hello Kitty guitars, that's a group which Squier is keen to sell its guitars to. Siegle mentions girlrocknation.com, Fender's effort to motivate and inspire more girls to play more (ideally Squier and Fender) guitars. Avril Lavigne is seen as a perfect role model. "She reaches a young, young, young demographic of primarily females," Siegle says. "They buy her perfume, they buy her Abbey Dawn clothing line, and all at affordable price-points – which is exactly where Squier comes in."

Siegle says he likes the fact that, in his toolbox of brands, Squier is a special case. "I can do some pretty amazing things with it, very economically, with some amazing guitars. A Squier is a Fender guitar that we can bend the rules on. We can't do that with Fender, because with Fender we have to stay pretty traditional and pretty conservative, otherwise people get offended. We can blur those lines with Squier. We can step on our own toes if we want to."

Discussions with Lavigne began. If she woke up with a new guitar idea, she would call Siegle. "'I want a purple sparkle acoustic.' We can do that. 'I want skull and crossbone inlays. And then I want the body with the Abbey Dawn logo.' You have to let the artist think out loud, let them think to the core. Gradually, I get to know what the model needs to be – so we start building the guitar without doing appointments. We do mockups, and we send stuff back and forth."

It's a matter of narrowing down what's required, Siegle explains. Soon, they decided on a Telecaster and that it needed to be simple and practical, without multiple buttons and switches. So they stripped it right down. "You have to ask the right questions. When she picks up a guitar, what's the first thing she does? Well, if there's a tone knob, she turns it all the way up. OK, that tells me she doesn't need a tone knob. Does she use her volume control? Some artists, like Pete Wentz on his bass, don't use a volume control: it's full blast

2008 Classic Vibe Duo-Sonic Desert Sand

SQUIER ELECTRICS

(RE)CREATING THAT CLASSIC VIBE

■ **Classic Vibe** was a new series starting in 2008 designed to recall the quality and vintage appeal of the original Japanese Squier models of the early 80s. These new Chinese-made models certainly had the right vibe: shown here are the 50s Strat (main guitar), a 50s Duo-Sonic (*opposite, top*), and, in the 2010 catalogue (*below*), a bound-body Telecaster Custom. Two new Squier signature models saw Telecasters for **Avril Lavigne** (*above*) and **Deryck Whibley** (*left*).

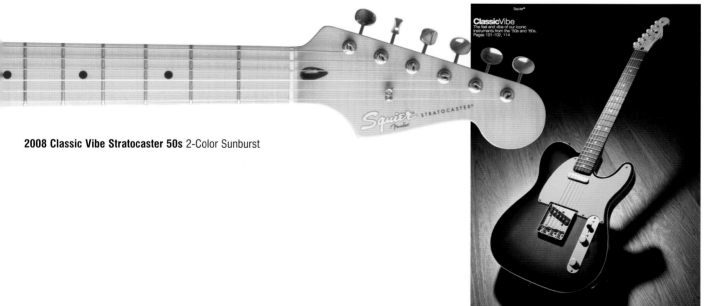

2008 Classic Vibe Stratocaster 50s 2-Color Sunburst

all the time. I didn't think she'd be that way, and she wasn't. She does use her volume control. OK, so one volume knob. We figured what the base model would be, and then we went to the cosmetic thing."

At the end of the back-and-forth process, many mock-ups later, Squier had a distinctive Avril Lavigne Tele to add to the line in 2007. It was complete with single humbucker, plus volume control, three-way coil-splitter, and input jack on the control plate. It had Lavigne's star logo on an otherwise marker-free fingerboard, her signature in the customary Fender position on the 'ball' of the headstock, and an individual black-and-white checkerboard-pattern pickguard on a black body.

Outsiders always want to know what the musician makes from a signature model. "While some of the artists make a pretty decent chunk of change from this, it's about giving back to the fans," Siegle insists. "It's like a co-branding arrangement, which is important to the integrity of our brand and our artists' brands. It's not like oh, this artist is big, here's ten million dollars, sign on the dotted line, and we're going to build a thousand of these guitars and you get ten free ones ... and see you later. When your first meeting is your last meeting and everything else is done mechanically, that's just sleazy bullshit. We don't work like that."[118]

Squier's June 2008 pricelist summed up a well-defined and impressive set of instruments: a Chinese Bullet Strat With Tremolo ($179.99); Indonesian Mini ($179.99), Hello Kitty Mini ($249.99), and Mini Player with built-in amp/speaker ($249.99); Chinese Affinity Strat and Strat HSS ($249.99) and Affinity Tele ($269.99); Indonesian Standard Strat, Standard Strat HSS, and Black & Chrome Standard Strat ($349.99), and Standard Tele and Black & Chrome Standard Tele ($349.99); Indonesian Hello Kitty Strat ($349.99); Chinese Vintage Modified Tele Custom and Custom II ($379.99) and Tele Thinline ($479.99), and Indian Vintage Modified Strat and Strat HSS ($499.99) and Tele SH and SSH ($499.99); Indonesian Deluxe Strat and Hot Rails Strat ($449.99); Chinese Jagmaster ($449.99); Indonesian Avril Lavigne Tele ($449.99) and Deryck Whibley Tele ($479.99); Indonesian Obey Graphic Strat and Tele ($449.99); Chinese Classic Vibe Duo-Sonic ($479.99) and Classic Vibe Strat 50s, Strat 60s, and Tele 50s ($499.99).

John 5, guitarist with Rob Zombie and a continually surprising artist in his own right, is a keen student of Fender history with an extensive collection of Telecasters. Now he's become part of that history himself, as the first musician to be honoured with signature models in all possible permutations – and, naturally, they're all Tele-based. He's had Fender-brand models from the Custom Shop, the Corona factory, and the Mexico factory, and in 2009 he completed the set with a Squier J5 Tele.

"When I talked to fans, the biggest complaint I got about guitars is that they're so expensive," John 5 says. Most people can't afford a several-thousand-dollar guitar, he says. "My main guitar is a black model that I use all the time, which Alex Perez built for me, an incredible guitar. So I said let's make a Squier version of that, something that everyone can afford, but really great quality." Squier's team got together with him and made a replica of that main guitar. It's one of Squier's Chinese-made models, and as John 5 says, listing at $599.99, it was priced to sell. "Squier did such a great job: it's great looking, with chrome all over it."

He says he's played the Squier on stage, and he's used it in the studio for doubling. So what's the difference between the Squier and his main guitar? "To be a thousand percent honest with you, the only thing that I can tell, really – because the neck is the same, it's got the same finish, everything – the only difference is the pickups. So I just change the pair of humbuckers to DiMarzios, and it's the same guitar. It's got binding, it's got the chrome pickguard, the chrome decal, everything. The only difference that I can tell is the pickups. Oh, and where it says Squier, mine says Fender."

As a collector, he's close to achieving his goal of owning a Fender Tele from every year, right from the start in 1951 up to 1980. For his own models, he chops around Bigsbys and pickups and the black-and-chrome look, but they're still Teles at heart. "I always think that the Telecaster, as our first solidbody electric guitar, is the greatest guitar in the world. They should stop making any other kind of guitar and just make the Telecaster. That's how strongly I feel about it."

What he found peculiar at first, given the model's versatility, was that hardly anyone in heavy rock played a Tele. "What's the problem with these people, I wondered? I wanted my guitar to be able to scream through the loudest amps, and I wanted to be able to play country with it and jazz with it, to have it be an all-around guitar. The Les Pauls can do that, but they can't really get that twang, they can't get that *thing*. I really think my Tele can do that, and – it's not because of me, I'm not taking credit for this at all – but I see a lot more heavy artists playing Telecasters now. After I started doing it, I saw Jim Root from Slipknot playing one, and I think I saw Tom Morello playing my signature model with his new band, Street Sweeper Social Club. It's like one of my kids, the Telecaster, you know? I'm passionate about it."[119]

Squier added a Simon Neil Strat in 2009, a signature model for the frontman of Britain's Biffy Clyro, for sale only in Europe. Now that Squier dabbled quite seriously with signature models – something that in the past had always been the preserve of Fender – it made sense for a brand with a worldwide production base to look beyond Anglo-American music and find other musicians who might make worthy endorsers. The idea had presented itself to Richard McDonald at a sales conference for Fender's Asian distributors in Hong Kong around 2004.

The subject of local musicians arose, and it was plain to McDonald that these guitarists, whom he'd never heard of, were huge in their own countries. It didn't take much of a leap – certainly not in the company of these businessmen who pushed the potential of such an idea – to consider local signature models that could be sold locally. "They started coming up with these artists," McDonald recalls, "and I started approving

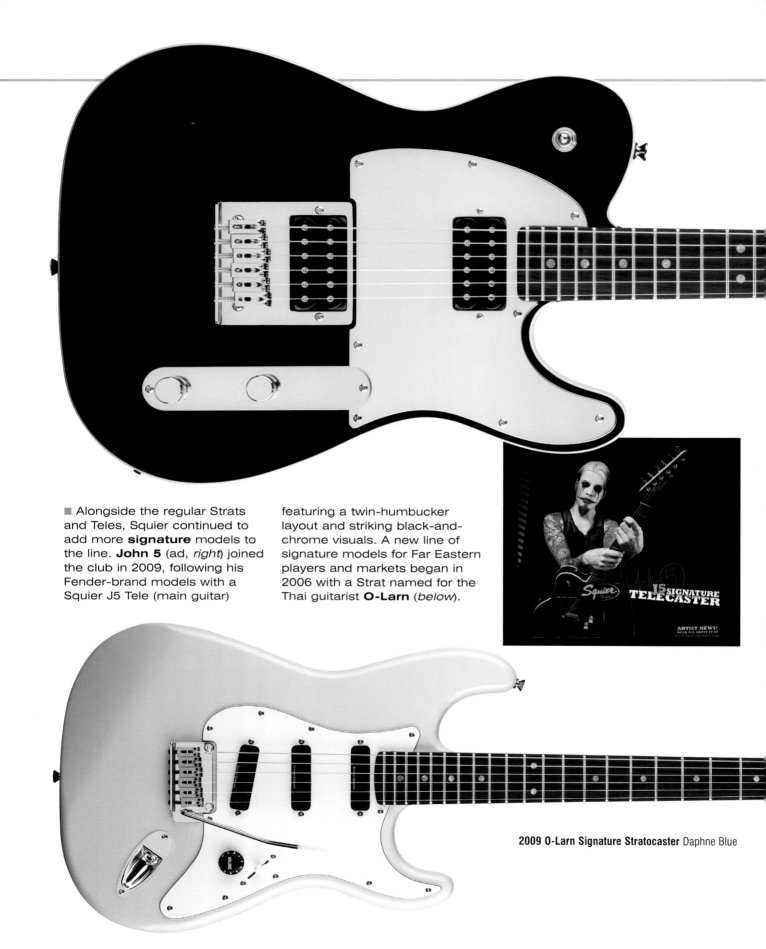

■ Alongside the regular Strats and Teles, Squier continued to add more **signature** models to the line. **John 5** (ad, *right*) joined the club in 2009, following his Fender-brand models with a Squier J5 Tele (main guitar) featuring a twin-humbucker layout and striking black-and-chrome visuals. A new line of signature models for Far Eastern players and markets began in 2006 with a Strat named for the Thai guitarist **O-Larn** (*below*).

2009 O-Larn Signature Stratocaster Daphne Blue

114

SQUIER ELECTRICS

SIGN IN, SQUIER

■ A red signature Strat hit European stores in 2009 for **Simon Neil** of Biffy Clyro (ad, *below left*). Meanwhile, countless guitarists loved and played their Squiers, including pros like **Chuck Prophet** (*below*).

2009 J5 Telecaster Black

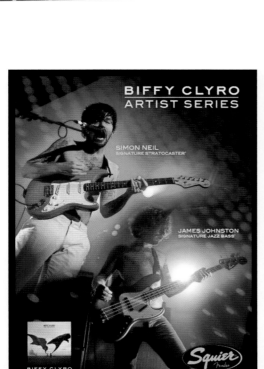

them. We'd do international artist models that are meaningful for a particular market, and they'd be Squiers, so they're affordable for the customer. It made total sense: local players to inspire and create a local sense of belonging. Frankly, they don't give a shit about Zakk Wylde. They might know Jimi Hendrix. But things that translate in the United States don't necessarily mean anything in Europe, and they definitely get watered down by the time you're in southern Asia."[120]

The first of these local artist models was the Squier O-Larn Signature Strat, launched in 2006 and for sale only in Thailand. Fender's Thai distributor, Beh Ngiep Seng Musical Instruments in Bangkok, argued that O-Larn was the local rock god worthy of a signature guitar. O-Larn was big in the early-70s rock scene in Thailand and is regarded there with affection as a player who's matured gracefully and can still draw the crowds. Next came the delightfully named Sham Kamikaze, another local hero. His signature Strat, with reverse headstock and reverse-angle bridge pickup, for sale only in Malaysia, appeared in 2009.

The latest member of what Squier calls its Regional Artist Program is Ehsaan Noorani, an Indian guitarist who came to fame through his work on Bollywood films. He'd studied at the Guitar Institute of Technology in Los Angeles in 1985 and returned to India in '86, working in Mumbai as a studio musician, mainly on commercials, for which he began to compose music.

"From there I got into this whole film thing," Noorani says, "and I formed the band Shankar Ehsaan Loy, with my two partners, in 1997. I'm basically a blues guitar player, and I've always been doing a bit of that, too, with a band, playing clubs. But with Shankar Ehsaan Loy, we perform our film music a lot. So I'm doing ... well, I don't know how many gigs a year here in India. And we were on tour in the USA last year, playing nine cities. So there's a lot of stuff happening." At the last count, Noorani and his band have contributed to over 40 Bollywood soundtracks. *Rock On!!* from 2008 – "probably India's first rock film," he says – is the one to listen to, Noorani suggests, to get an idea of his abilities as a player.

Noorani bought his first Fender in 1981, a 70s Strat. "Around the time I started playing and formed my first band in the early 80s," he says, "there were only a few people who had Fenders, and you were in complete awe of those guys ... because they actually owned Fender Stratocasters. It was very difficult to get one here in India. The only way you could was if somebody brought one back in his baggage and sold it to you – and you'd pay a fair amount over the actual price."

He moved to a PRS, which saw him through the 80s. Then, around 1993, he met Jasbeer Singh, who had by now become the sole distributor for Fender in India through his company Reemal Investrade in Mumbai. "That was amazing," Noorani says, "because it meant I could finally get Fenders. I could choose a model I wanted and not just depend on somebody carrying it back. So I went through quite a few guitars, including an American Standard and one of the Mexican Fenders. Then Sean Morris and Jon Gold from Fender came down to India to see what the Fender presence was like, to take the dealerships to the next level. I flew down to Delhi to meet them, and I was very excited."

The meeting went well – Noorani even managed to get them all on national TV to talk about Fender guitars, which must have impressed the visitors. Morris and Gold offered to make Noorani a Custom Shop model. "It wasn't an endorsement," he says, "but just to show their gratitude to me for doing so much for Fender in India. John Cruz made me the guitar, and it was the prototype for what I'm using now."

Next, Jasbeer Singh talked to Fender about a Noorani signature model, in the wake of the O-Larn and Sham Kamikaze Squiers. There was a lot of back-and-forth on the design, Noorani says. "Most Indian guitar players have small hands: we're not as large as Caucasian people, we're smaller people. Very often you'd pick up an American Standard, say, and you'd find you're struggling a bit with the width of the fretboard. I said we ought to go for a standard width but a very shallow neck, because that would really help us wrap our fingers around."

Noorani opted for an unusual humbucker/single-coil/humbucker configuration. "The middle pickup is great to use in combination, but I find it a waste for anything else – a purely personal thing. So I said let's combine the bridge pickup and the neck pickup in humbucker mode so you get that classic centre sound, like you'd get in a Les Paul, for B.B. King-style blues. I really like the sound of humbuckers on a Strat. It doesn't sound quite Fender and it doesn't sound quite Gibson: it's got this in-between thing, which is fabulous. The guitar is wired so that the second and fourth positions give me that typical Stratocaster cluck – which of course you can't do without," he laughs.

Squier seemed a natural choice of brand. "I've got to be realistic about the scene in India," Noorani says. "If it was Fender, either USA or Mexico, the price would be fairly expensive for the average guitar player to afford. I could go for the Custom Shop … and I'd probably be the only one who'd buy it in India. The guys at Squier said it would be made at the same factory in China that makes the Classic Vibe guitars, and they are a great success as far as Squier is concerned. They said check it out, of course, and if I didn't like it they could keep working on it. But when I finally played the approved model, I just couldn't believe it. I couldn't believe this Squier was so resonant, so comfortable to play. Sonically, it was as good as anything else I've played."[121]

He's kept a close eye on how the Squier Ehsaan Noorani Strat has done since its launch in the early months of 2011. He relies on social networking to keep him up to date and works hard with promo workshops and various other means to maintain the momentum. When we spoke in May that year, he was confident that the first batch would soon be sold out in India and that a further thousand would be along soon.

Chris Gill at Squier is confident that the Noorani model, and the O-Larn and Kamikaze signatures before it, marks an important new step for the brand. "Like with everything," Gill says, "the world has become a big melting pot, and I think at some

■ Squier's Regional Artist Program moved forward with a Strat (main guitar) for the Indian guitarist **Ehsaan Noorani** (*right*), known for his Bollywood film music and band Shankar Ehsaan Loy. Meanwhile, Squier developed the **Classic Vibe** series (Tele Thinline, *below*) and **Vintage Modified** series (Jaguar, *opposite*). In 2012, as Squier's catalogue ranged from the cheapest **Bullet** models (group picture, *opposite*) to the top-priced Classic Vibe models, the brand enjoyed a successful 30th birthday.

2010 Classic Vibe Telecaster Thinline Natural

2011 Ehsaan Noorani Stratocaster Transparent Green

SQUIER ELECTRICS

**2011 Vintage
Modified Jaguar HH**
Fiesta Red

point it might make sense strategically to offer some of these products elsewhere. But initially, what we want to do is partner with a distributor and have them benefit directly into their own economy. However, if you look at Ehsaan Noorani, for example, who last year did a huge tour of the USA and Canada and hit all the major metro marketplaces with high Indian populations, there might well be an opportunity to offer a guitar like that outside India."[122]

One more recent development for Squier – although one that was some time in development – was a real-guitar controller for the *Rock Band 3* video game. The Squier By Fender Stratocaster Guitar & Controller, to give it its full name, was finally launched in 2011. The project had been started around 2004, when Justin Norvell was still at Squier. Why did it take so long? "We had to create a technology that allowed the game to understand where you are on the fretboard, so it could sense where you are and teach you," Norvell says. "That was hard work."

The original controllers that came with *Rock Band* were guitar-like objects with five simple pushbuttons. Norvell's plan, in collaboration with the game's creator, Harmonix, was to make a real electric guitar that you could actually play, and on which, through the game, you could use to learn how to play. "People had very quickly got to mastering the game and being able to play Yngwie Malmsteen songs with the buttons," Norvell says. "But they needed a new challenge. We wanted a way to make the game a gateway for people to actually learn how to play." In fact, the $279.99 Squier gaming guitar may have come too late, because Harmonix is not currently developing new versions of *Rock Band*. But there are still plenty of gamers out there who continue to play it.

Today, 30 years since the start of Squier, the brand is in better shape then ever. Given the sometimes turbulent history we've unravelled, it's something of a shock that Squier has managed to end up in such a healthy state. It's endured a lot of blows along the way, and it's survived multiple shifts in purpose as one manager went in one direction and then the next would take the opposite tack.

Dan Smith was right there in the thick of it from day one, and these days he's busy enjoying his retirement. "Squier was a brand name we more or less came up with as a means of trying to sell offshore-produced guitars and basses," he says, "while having the least impact on a struggling US manufacturing base. In retrospect, I'm more than a little surprised it's survived a myriad of marketing approaches, going from being a potentially temporary fix, through various flights of full-line fantasy, and finally becoming a solid brandname that's weathered an up-and-down market for three decades. It's amazing to me. Fender had only been in the guitar business slightly more than 30 years when I got there in 1981. And now a book to mark Squier's 30th anniversary. Who'd have thought?"[123]

Bill Mendello, another man in there at the beginning of Squier in the 80s, retired from his job as Fender CEO in 2010. He, too, is full of wonder at the resilience of Squier.

"The company ran from one very critical decision that we made back in 1981, which was that we were going to compete through the entire range. That has really led to where Fender is today. Had we made the decision 30 years ago that we were just going to compete on the high-end, that we were going to be a niche company, or Fender only, it would have been a very different company.

"We made the decision that we were going to compete and that it wasn't critical that everything we made had the name Fender on it," Mendello continues. "Most people look at Squier as a low-end Fender. It is, but to us it was a way to compete in the world. It's not only a low-price brand, it's a value brand. We felt competitiveness was critical to our success. For a long time we tracked it, and we were selling more Squier units than any electric guitar brand in the world. It's probably still true today."[124]

The January 2011 Squier pricelist offered the following models: an Indonesian Mini ($179.99); a Chinese Bullet Strat with Tremolo and a Bullet Strat with Tremolo HSS ($199.99); a Chinese Affinity Strat, Strat HSS, and Tele ($279.99); an Indonesian Standard Strat, Strat HSS, and Tele ($379.99); a Chinese Standard Black & Chrome Strat, Strat HSS, and Tele ($379.99); a Chinese Vintage Modified Tele Custom and Custom II ($399.99), and Tele Thinline, Jaguar HH, and Jazzmaster (($499.99); an Indonesian Avril Lavigne Tele ($479.99); a Chinese Jagmaster ($479.99); an Indonesian Deluxe Strat and Hot Rails Strat ($479.99); an Indonesian Deryck Whibley Telecaster ($499.99); a Chinese Classic Vibe Duo-Sonic ($529.99), two Strats and a Tele ($549.99), and a Tele Custom and Thinline ($599.99); an Indian Vintage Modified Strat, Strat HSS, Tele SH, and Tele SSH ($549.99); and a Chinese J5 Telecaster ($599.99).

That line-up reflected how confident Squier has become in recent years, at last settling down with its own separate and secure identity within the Fender fold. And while the Kittys, the Obeys, the Whibleys, and the Nooranis all brought welcome attention to the brand, Squier's real-world purpose today is to provide good, playable, everyday guitars at affordable prices for ordinary guitarists.

It's hard to believe from today's perspective how much the original team back in the early 80s worried about the effect that a non-US-made Fender might have on the firm's reputation and future. The Squier brand was adopted to offset some of that worry. Richard McDonald, at the time of writing senior vice president of marketing Fender brands, believes that a guitar's place of origin is irrelevant today. "The generation of buyers now are not asking where a guitar was made. They're not looking for the mark that says 'Made In USA' or 'Made In Mexico' and they're not prejudiced against things made in China or wherever."

It's a generational phenomenon, says 53-year-old McDonald. "To my dad, Japan equalled crap. My brother is ten years older than me, and I can't see him ever buying a product made in Vietnam. But we have a proliferation of imported goods now: all your cool electronics stuff is coming from these other countries. And we've taught them to make guitars! People like Dan Smith, Mike Lewis, myself, and others, these luthiers and guitar-centric guys have spent years in Asia teaching them to do it right. When we have a Squier guitar like a Classic Vibe or a Vintage Modified, you're looking at a magnificent value, a guitar that just blows you away. It doesn't matter where it comes from any more. Country-of-origin issues are gone, in my view."[125]

Chris Gill, at the head of Squier as it hits its remarkable 30th anniversary, is full of hope for the decades that lie ahead for the brand. "The future," he says, "is in tilling the soil, developing new relationships with artists, always being on the front end of musical trends and what's happening, and continuing to bring value-packed instruments to our consumers, whether that's a $100 guitar or a $399 guitar." Gill wants to continue to put the iconic Fender designs before new eyes and, as he puts it, to "bring new followers to the church of Fender". If you haven't got the bucks for a Custom Shop guitar, he says, or even a regular Fender guitar, then Squier wants to find you a place.

"This is what's made Squier very successful over the years," says Gill, "and that's where we want to keep going. You see it every day. Here's the guy who just made the Classic Vibe purchase, maybe as a backup instrument, and there's somebody else who's bought one because they were drooling over a vintage guitar but, gosh, they just don't have the money for it. And when they make the purchase and they're satisfied with it, they go online and they tell everybody about it. They say this Squier is every bit as good as something way more expensive. That's what I mean by giving people the best guitar I can for whatever they can afford."[126]

Squier is like Texas, Richard McDonald says. "Texas is part of the United States, but it's so big and so robust and has such an identity of its own that, OK, it is one of the 50 states, but it's *Texas*. It's kind of the same thing with Squier. Squier is part of Fender, but it's *Squier*."[127]

Endnotes

1   Tom Wheeler & Steve Rosen *Guitar Player* February 1979
2   Author's interview February 4 1992
3   *The Music Trades* January 1965
4   *Up Beat* July 1981
5   Author's interview June 3 2011
6   Tom Wheeler *Guitar Player* May 1978
7   *The Music Trades* June 1973
8   Author's interview June 3 2011
9   *Electronics & Music Maker* February 1982
10   Author's interview May 11 2011
11   *Billboard* November 13 1982
12   Author's interview May 27 2011
13   Author's interview February 4 1992
14   Author's interview May 11 2011
15   Author's interview June 2 2005
16   Author's interview February 4 1992
17   Author's interview May 27 2011
18   Author's interview May 11 2011
19   *Japan Music Trades* English Readers Edition April 1982
20   Peter Cook *Music World* April 1982
21   *Japan Music Trades* English Readers Edition June 1982
22   Author's interview May 11 2011
23   Author's interview May 13 2011
24   Author's interview May 11 2011
25   *Japan Music Trades* March 1984
26   *Japan Music Trades* March 1984
27   Author's interview May 11 2011
28   Author's interview May 11 2011
29   *Japan Music Trades* August 1983
30   Author's interview May 27 2011
31   Author's interview February 4 1992
32   *Musician* July 1982
33   Author's interview May 4 2011
34   Author's interview May 11 2011
35   Author's interview May 19 2011
36   Author's interview May 11 2011
37   Author's interview May 11 2011
38   Author's interview May 27 2011
39   Victor Carroll Squier, unpublished autobiographical paper, 1944
40   Carlotta Parsons, unpublished Victor Carroll Squier biographical notes, undated
41   Victor Carroll Squier, unpublished autobiographical paper, 1944
42   Mary Steffek Blaske *The Herald*, Greenfield Village & Henry Ford Museum, Fall 1978
43   Carlotta Parsons, unpublished Victor Carroll Squier biographical notes, undated
44   Author's correspondence June 12 2011
45   Author's correspondence July 8 2011
46   Author's interview May 31 2011
47   Author's correspondence July 11 2011
48   Author's correspondence June 3 2011
49   Paul Colbert *Melody Maker* July 10 1982
50   Author's interview May 17 2011
51   Author's interview May 27 2011
52   Author's interview May 19 2011
53   Author's interview May 17 2011
54   Author's interview May 13 2011
55   Author's correspondence May 28 2011 via Nick Sugimoto
56   *Japan Music Trades* English Readers Edition December 1982
57   *Japan Music Trades* November 1982
58   Author's interview May 11 2011
59   *Guitar Player* December 1983
60   Author's interview February 4 1992
61   *San Francisco Chronicle* January 15 1985
62   Author's interview May 11 2011

63   Author's interview June 3 2011

64   Author's interview February 11 1985

65   Author's interview May 11 2011

66   *The Music Trades* April 1985

67   Author's interview May 11 2011

68   Author's interview May 11 2011

69   Author's interview June 3 2011

70   Author's interview May 13 2011

71   Author's interview May 11 2011

72   Author's correspondence July 7 2011

73   *Japan Music Trades* August 1983

74   Author's interview May 11 2011

75   Author's interview June 3 2011

76   Author's interview November 21 1997 & May 10 2011

77   Author's interview July 29 2011

78   Author's interview November 21 1997 & May 10 2011

79   Chris Kraul *Los Angeles Times* September 5 1997

80   Author's interview November 21 1997 & May 10 2011

81   Author's interview May 3 2011

82   Author's interview June 8 2011

83   Author's interview May 10 2011

84   Author's interview June 3 2011

85   Author's interview May 12 2011

86   Author's interview May 10 2011

87   Author's interview May 19 2011

88   Author's interview May 12 2011

89   Author's interview May 10 2011

90   Author's interview May 10 2011

91   Author's interview May 19 2011

92   Author's interview April 27 2011

93   *Fender Frontline* 2003

94   Author's interview April 27 2011

95   Author's interview April 27 2011

96   Author's interview May 9 2011

97   Author's interview April 27 2011

98   Author's interview May 9 2011

99   Author's interview April 27 2011

100   Art Thompson *Guitar Player* October 2004

101   Author's interview April 27 2011

102   Author's interview May 19 2011

103   Author's interview May 20 2011

104   acapella.harmony-central.com, September 14 2009

105   Author's interview April 27 2011

106   Author's interview April 18 2011

107   Author's interview May 9 2011

108   *Newsweek* November 27 2005

109   Author's interview May 9 2011

110   6767.com/2011/02/28/hello-kitty-hello-dave-navarro, February 28 2011

111   Author's interview July 12 2011

112   Author's interview May 19 2011

113   Author's interview July 12 2011

114   Author's interview May 3 2011

115   Author's interview May 11 2011

116   Author's interview June 3 2011

117   Author's interview May 12 2011

118   Author's interview May 26 2011

119   Author's interview May 24 2011

120   Author's interview May 19 2011

121   Author's interview May 5 2011

122   Author's interview April 18 2011

123   Author's interview May 11 2011

124   Author's interview June 3 2011

125   Author's interview May 19 2011

126   Author's interview April 18 2011

127   Author's interview May 19 2011

THE
REFERENCE
LISTING

REFERENCE LISTING

We've designed this Reference Listing to help you identify Squier electric guitars made between 1982 and 2011. As with the rest of this book, there is no coverage of acoustic guitars or bass guitars and we've excluded models made uniquely for the Japanese domestic market. So, we assume that you're looking at a guitar or a picture of a guitar and you want to work out what it is.

THE HEADSTOCK: INSTANT INFORMATION

First of all, you need to get as much information as you can from the guitar itself, and the best place for you to start your search is on the instrument's headstock. With Squier guitars, it represents an important source of information. Potentially, it can tell you what the guitar is, where it was made, and when it was produced.

Brand

The brandname is on the face of the guitar's headstock and it simply confirms that the guitar is a Squier, although the Fender brandname is also usually present. On the earliest Squier guitars, produced during 1982, a large Fender logo was accompanied by a small "Squier Series" logo on the end or 'ball' of the headstock face. This layout was soon amended to a large "Squier" brand logo, usually above, or adjacent to, a small "by Fender" logo. This layout is still in use, although some Korean and Mexican-made Squiers produced in the 90s employed the original arrangement with similar big "Fender" and small "Squier Series" logos but not in the original font.

Model

When present, the name of the model is usually to be found on the instrument's headstock face, near the brand logo. For example: "Stratocaster", "Telecaster", "Bullet", "Venus", and so on. Despite the numerous additional names that you'll see in the listings, bear in mind that Squiers (like Fenders) rarely give the *full* model name on the guitar itself. Most often it's simply "Stratocaster", "Telecaster", and so on, even if it is in fact a Standard Double Fat Strat or a Vintage Modified Telecaster Custom.

Series

When present, this is usually on the headstock face, located apart from the brand logo and model name and often on the 'ball'. For example: "Affinity Series", "Pro Tone Series", "Vista Series", and so on. (See also *Series Name* in the dating section, page 150.)

Source

When present, the manufacturing source is usually shown on the instrument's headstock face or back, although on some guitars you can find it on the neck heel or on the neck-plate. It can tell you where the guitar was made. For example: "Crafted in China", "Crafted in Indonesia", "Made in Japan", and so on.

Serial number

The serial number is usually on the headstock face or back, although on some instruments it is on the neck heel (the rear flat section near the body joint) or the neck-plate (the metal plate on the back of the body at the neck joint). Information coded into the serial number can sometimes confirm the guitar's country of origin and provide an approximate production year. (For much more information, see *Serial Numbers* in the dating section, pages 150–153.)

What next?

Now that you know more about your guitar, you'll want to look it up in more detail in the listings that follow. The three main sections within the Reference Listing are:

Stratocasters (pages 127–135)
Telecasters (pages 135–139)
Other Models (pages 139–149)

These are followed by a brief look at Squier-related brands (page 149), a section on dating that includes detailed serial-number keys (pages 150–153), and a model chronology or timeline (pages 153–155).

Within the Stratocaster and Telecaster sections, we've grouped the models into what we term 'Regular' and 'Revised' versions.

'Regular' models are what we determine as models with established, normal-design specifications. If you're looking at a 'Regular' Stratocaster or Telecaster – that's one with the standard pickups and controls, a traditional look, and nothing out of the ordinary – then there's not much more to be said. We've given some general clues to period and style, but generally what you see is what you've got.

'Revised' models are the alternative examples, those with significant departures from the standard specs. Within the 'Revised' Stratocaster section and 'Revised' Telecaster section we have further divided these models, based on their various pickup configurations.

The section headed Other Models includes those Squiers not directly derived from the Stratocaster or from the Telecaster.

In all these sections and sub-sections, each guitar is listed in the alphabetical order of the model name, usually in accordance with Fender's published catalogues and pricelists. Where a person's name is the model name, then the forename, rather than the surname, determines the alphabetical order. For example, the Avril Lavigne Telecaster will be found under A, not L.

UNDERSTANDING THE ENTRIES

At the head of each instrument entry is the model name in bold type, and in the case of the Other Models this is followed by a body shape reference number, in brackets, for more details of which see that section.

Next in each listing is a year or range of years indicating the production period of the particular guitar. It should be stressed that these dates are approximate, as manufacturing spans are often hard to pinpoint with total accuracy. The dates shown are based on our extensive research and on official data supplied by Fender, and therefore they represent the best information available.

Following the year or years is a single sentence *in italic type* describing the specific model's most identifiable unique features. This brief summary is intended to help you recognise an instrument quickly and provides further confirmation with the more detailed information shown in the accompanying specification points that make up the remainder of each entry. In a few cases we have insufficient facts for a full entry, and when this is so, the information is preceded by the line *Limited information available, as follows:* .

For some guitars, a sentence below the heading will state "Similar to ... , except:". This is a reference to another model entry, and the specification points that follow indicate only the differences between the two.

Most guitar entries then include a list of bullet points that relate to the particular model's specifications and other relevant features. In listed order, these points refer to the following components:

- Model series (when applicable and shown on the instrument).
- Neck, fingerboard; frets; truss-rod adjuster; tuners; string-guides; headstock; nut; neck-plate.
- Body; finish colour.
- Pickups.
- Controls; output jack.
- Pickguard.
- Bridge.
- Metalwork finish.
Any other information.
Part Number (*see page 153 for more information*)
Production country or countries

To avoid needless repetition, we consider certain features as common to all Squier models, and so these are not shown in every entry. Unless stated otherwise, you can always assume the following:

Bolt-on neck.
Fingerboard with dot position-markers.
Twenty-five-and-a-half-inch (648mm) scale length.
Twenty-one frets.
Metal tuner buttons.
Recognised Fender headstock shape.
Four-screw neck-plate.
Solid contoured offset-double-cutaway body.
Single-coil pickups.
Nickel or chrome-plat-ed metalwork.

REGULAR STRATOCASTERS

Since the Squier brand was introduced in 1982, Fender has produced many versions of what we define as the 'Regular' Squier Stratocaster. All examples have "Stratocaster" or "Strat" on the headstock. The headstock can also provide pointers to a specific series, to tcountry of origin, and to production date, as explained opposite under The Headstock: Instant Information. All Stratocasters have Body Shape 1 – see page 139.

'REGULAR' STRATOCASTER 1982–current

- Maple neck, rosewood or maple fingerboard; 21 or 22 frets; truss-rod adjuster at body or at headstock; one or two string-guides; "Stratocaster" or "Strat" on small (vintage-style) or enlarged (70s-style) headstock; headstock face natural or colour; four or three-screw neck-plate.
- Solid, contoured, offset-double-cutaway body; sunburst or colours.
- Three six-polepiece pickups (bridge pickup angled).
- Three controls (volume, two tone) and three or five-way selector, all on pickguard; output jack in body front.
- Laminate or single-layer plastic or anodised metal pickguard.
- Two or six-pivot bridge/vibrato unit; or six-saddle small bridge with through-body stringing; or six-saddle small bridge/tailpiece.
- Nickel, chrome, gold, or black-plated metalwork.

* Some 'Regular' Stratocasters have a series name on the headstock:
"Affinity Series" (1997–current)
"Bullet Series" (1994–97)
"California Series" (2003–current)
"Pro Tone Series" (1996–98)
"Silver Series" (1992–94)
"Squier Series" with large Fender logo (1982 Japan, 1992–94 Korea, 1994–96 Mexico)
"Standard Series" (1999–current)
* Some 'Regular' Stratocasters are known by a series name that is not on the guitar but is used in catalogues, ads, pricelists, etc. These series include:
Classic (1993–94)
Classic Vibe (2008–current)
Deluxe (2004–current)
Popular (UK; simply 'Squier Stratocaster' US), aka 'SQ', 'big headstock' (1983–84)
Satin Trans (2005–07)
Standard (1985–99)
Tradition/Traditional (1996)
U.S. Standard (1991–92)
Vintage Modified (2007–current)
'57 Stratocaster / '62 Stratocaster (1982–84)
China, India, Indonesia, Japan, Korea, Mexico, USA

REVISED STRATOCASTERS

Listed next are the models we regard as Fender's altered and adapted versions of the 'Regular' Squier Stratocaster (for which see the earlier *Regular Stratocasters* section). These 'Revised' Stratocasters incorporate significant visible changes to cosmetics, construction, and/or components. For ease of reference we've divided them into sections based on pickup configurations. They are arranged in the following order:

H   One humbucker (at bridge).
HH   Two humbuckers.
HSH   Two humbuckers and one single-coil (in centre).
HSS   One humbucker (at bridge) and two single-coils.
SSS   Three single-coils, or three single-coil-size humbuckers.

REVISED STRATOCASTERS: H

One humbucker (at bridge).

CONTEMPORARY STRATOCASTER H 1985–88 *Black-face headstock, no pickguard, one black humbucker.*
- Maple neck, rosewood fingerboard; 24.75-inch scale; truss-rod adjuster at body; two string-guides; black-face headstock.
- Body black or red.
- One black coverless humbucker (at bridge).
- One control (volume) on body; side-mounted output jack.
- Six-pivot bridge/vibrato unit.
025-4700
Japan

HELLO KITTY STRAT 2006–09 *Hello Kitty cartoon pickguard.*
- "Affinity Series" on headstock.
- Maple neck, maple fingerboard; truss-rod adjuster at headstock; two string-guides; enlarged (70s-style) headstock.
- Body black or pink with Hello Kitty logo graphic on back.
- One white coverless humbucker (at bridge).
- One control (volume) on body; side-mounted output jack.
- Hello Kitty cartoon pickguard.
- Six-saddle small bridge with through-body stringing.
033-5005
Indonesia

ROLLING ROCK STRATOCASTER 2004 *Rolling Rock graphic on body front.*
- "Standard Series" on headstock.
- Maple neck, rosewood fingerboard; 22 frets; truss-rod adjuster at headstock; two string-guides; enlarged (70s-style) headstock.
- Body green only with Rolling Rock graphic on front.
- One black coverless humbucker (at bridge).
- One control (volume).
- Two-pivot bridge/vibrato unit.
032-2601
Indonesia

STRATOCASTER GUITAR & CONTROLLER 2011–current *22 six-section frets, seven game controller buttons.*
- Maple neck, polymer fingerboard; 22 six-section frets; truss-rod adjuster in side of heel; two string-guides.
- Body black only.
- One white plain-top humbucker (at bridge).
- One control (volume), seven game controller buttons, and string mute (at neck), all on pickguard; output jack in body front; side-mounted MIDI output.
- White plastic pickguard.
- Six-saddle bridge/tailpiece.
034-8000
Korea

TOM DELONGE STRATOCASTER 2002–03 *"Tom DeLonge" on neck-plate.*
- "Standard Series" on headstock.
- Maple neck, rosewood fingerboard; truss-rod adjuster at headstock; one string-guide; "Tom DeLonge" on neck-plate.
- Body black, green, or white.
- One white coverless humbucker (at bridge).
- One control (volume) on pickguard; output jack in body front.
- White laminate plastic pickguard.
- Six-saddle small bridge with through-body stringing.
031-8200
China

REVISED STRATOCASTERS: HH

Two humbuckers.

CONTEMPORARY STRATOCASTER HH 1985–87 *Black-face headstock, no pickguard, two black humbuckers.*
Similar to CONTEMPORARY STRATOCASTER H (see earlier listing in Revised Stratocasters: H), except:
- 22 frets; truss-rod adjuster at headstock.
- Two black coverless humbuckers.
- Two controls (volume, tone) and three-way selector, all on body.
027-4500
Japan

DETONATOR STRAT FSR 2007 *Metal pushbutton switch on pickguard.*
- "Affinity Series" on headstock.
- Maple neck, rosewood fingerboard; truss-rod adjuster at headstock; two string-guides; black-face enlarged (70s-style) headstock.
- Body black only.
- Two black coverless humbuckers.
- Two controls (volume, tone), three-way selector, and metal pushbutton switch, all on pickguard; output jack in body front.
- Black plastic pickguard.
- Six-pivot bridge/vibrato unit.
Factory Special Run.
032-2916
Indonesia

SATIN TRANS FAT STRATOCASTER HH 2005–07 *Satin-finish body, two metal-cover humbuckers, no pickguard, "Standard Series" on headstock.*
- ▓ "Standard Series" on headstock.
- ▓ Maple neck, rosewood fingerboard; 22 frets; truss-rod adjuster at headstock; two string-guides; enlarged (70s-style) headstock, face matches body colour.
- ▓ Body satin black, orange, or red.
- ▓ Two metal-cover humbuckers.
- ▓ Three controls (volume, two tone) and three-way selector, all on body; output jack in body front.
- ▓ Two-pivot bridge/vibrato unit.
032-1830
Indonesia

STANDARD DOUBLE FAT STRAT first version 1999–2000
Enlarged headstock, 21 frets, two white humbuckers.
- ▓ "Standard Series" on headstock.
- ▓ Maple neck, rosewood or maple fingerboard; truss-rod adjuster at headstock; two string-guides; enlarged (70s-style) headstock.
- ▓ Body sunburst or colours.
- ▓ Two white coverless humbuckers.
- ▓ Two controls (volume, tone) and three-way selector, all on pickguard; output jack in body front.
- ▓ White laminate plastic pickguard.
- ▓ Six-pivot bridge/vibrato unit.
032-1800 & 1802
China, Indonesia

STANDARD DOUBLE FAT STRAT second version 2000–07
Enlarged headstock, 22 frets, two black humbuckers.
Similar to STANDARD DOUBLE FAT STRAT first version (see previous listing), except:
- ▓ Maple neck, rosewood fingerboard only; 22 frets; headstock face matches certain body colours.
- ▓ Two black coverless humbuckers.
- ▓ Three controls (volume, two tone) and three-way selector.
- ▓ Black or black laminate plastic pickguard.
- ▓ Two-pivot bridge/vibrato unit.
032-1800
Indonesia

STANDARD DOUBLE FAT STRAT 7 HT seven-string
2000–02 *Enlarged seven-string headstock, 22 frets, two black humbuckers.*
Similar to STANDARD DOUBLE FAT STRAT second version (see earlier listing), except:
- ▓ "Stratocaster VII" on seven-string headstock.
- ▓ Body sunburst, black, or purple.
- ▓ Seven-saddle small bridge with through-body stringing.
032-1837
Indonesia

REVISED STRATOCASTERS: HSH
Two humbuckers and one single-coil (in centre).

EHSAAN NOORANI STRATOCASTER 2011–current *Ehsaan Noorani signature on headstock.*
- ▓ Maple neck, rosewood fingerboard; 22 frets; truss-rod adjuster at headstock; locking tuners; one string-guide; Ehsaan Noorani signature on headstock.
- ▓ Body with flame maple front; various colours.
- ▓ Two black coverless humbuckers and one white six-polepiece pickup in centre.
- ▓ Three controls (volume, two tone) and five-way selector, all on pickguard; output jack in body front.
- ▓ White pearl laminate plastic pickguard.
- ▓ Two-pivot bridge/vibrato unit.
Sold in India only.
030-1030
China

REVISED STRATOCASTERS: HSS
One humbucker (at bridge) and two single-coils.

AFFINITY FAT STRAT *See later listing for STRAT HSS.*

AFFINITY STRATOCASTER HSS *See later listing for STRAT HSS.*

BLACK & CHROME FAT STRAT 2005–current *Black body, chrome pickguard, one black humbucker and two black single-coils.*
Similar to BLACK & CHROME STANDARD STRATOCASTER (see later listing in Revised Stratocasters: SSS), except:
- ▓ One black coverless humbucker (at bridge) and two black six-polepiece pickups.
Also known as BLACK & CHROME STRATOCASTER HSS.
032-1703
China

BLACK & CHROME STRATOCASTER HSS *See previous listing for BLACK & CHROME FAT STRAT.*

CALIFORNIA FAT STRAT first version 2003–current *"Strat" and "California Series" on headstock, maple fingerboard, one humbucker and two single-coils, white pearl pickguard.*
- ▓ "California Series" on headstock.
- ▓ Maple neck, maple fingerboard; truss-rod adjuster at headstock; two string-guides.
- ▓ Body sunburst or colours.
- ▓ One white coverless humbucker (at bridge) and two white six-polepiece pickups.
- ▓ Three controls (volume, two tone) and five-way selector, all on pickguard; output jack in body front.
- ▓ White pearl laminate plastic pickguard.
- ▓ Six-pivot bridge/vibrato unit.
Sold in China only.
632-0502
China

CALIFORNIA FAT STRAT second version 2003–current *Strat and "California Series" on headstock, rosewood fingerboard, one humbucker and two single-coils, white laminate plastic pickguard.*
Similar to CALIFORNIA STRAT first version (see previous listing), except:
▪ Maple neck, rosewood fingerboard.
▪ White laminate plastic pickguard.
Sold in Australia and Latin America only.
633-0200
China.

CONTEMPORARY STRATOCASTER first version 1988–91
No pickguard, one black humbucker and two black single-coils, locking bridge/vibrato system.
▪ Maple neck, rosewood fingerboard; truss-rod adjuster at headstock; single-bar string-guide; locking nut.
▪ Body various colours.
▪ One black coverless humbucker (at bridge) and two black six-polepiece pickups.
▪ Three controls (volume, two tone) and five-way selector, all on body; side-mounted output jack.
▪ Two-pivot locking bridge/vibrato unit.
033-1000 & 133-1000
Korea

CONTEMPORARY STRATOCASTER second version
1992–94 *No pickguard, one black humbucker and two black single-coils, six-pivot bridge/vibrato unit.*
▪ Maple neck, maple fingerboard; truss-rod adjuster at headstock; two string-guides.
▪ Body black, red, or white.
▪ One black coverless humbucker (at bridge) and two black six-polepiece pickups.
▪ Three controls (volume, two tone) and five-way selector, all on body; side-mounted output jack.
▪ Six-pivot bridge/vibrato unit.
033-6002
Korea

CONTEMPORARY STRATOCASTER third version *See later listing for STANDARD FAT STRAT first version.*

CONTEMPORARY STRATOCASTER HSS 1986–88 *Black-face headstock, no pickguard, one black humbucker and two black single-coils.*
Similar to CONTEMPORARY STRATOCASTER H (see earlier listing in Revised Stratocasters: H), except:
▪ 22 frets; truss-rod adjuster at headstock.
▪ Body black, red, or white.
▪ One black coverless humbucker (at bridge) and two black six-polepiece pickups.
▪ Two controls (volume, tone) and three mini-switches, all on body.
027-6800
Japan

FAT STRAT *See later listing for STRAT HSS.*

FAT STRAT FSR first version 2001–07 *"Strat" and "Affinity Series" on black-face enlarged headstock, one black humbucker and two black single-coils, black pickguard, black-plated metalwork.*
Similar to STRAT HSS (see later listing), except:
▪ Black-face headstock.
▪ Body blue or red.
▪ One black coverless humbucker (at bridge) and two black six-polepiece pickups.
▪ Black plastic pickguard.
▪ Black-plated metalwork.
Factory Special Run, sold in Canada only.
031-0700
China.

FAT STRAT FSR second version 2006–07 *"Strat" and "Affinity Series" on enlarged headstock with face matching body colour, one white humbucker and two white single-coils, white pickguard.*
Similar to FAT STRAT FSR first version (previous listing), except:
▪ Headstock face matches body colour.
▪ Body black, red, or silver.
▪ One white coverless humbucker (at bridge) and two white six-polepiece pickups.
▪ White plastic pickguard.
Factory Special Run.
032-2906
Indonesia.

FAT STRAT MAPLE FSR 2001–07 *"Strat" and "Affinity Series" on enlarged headstock, maple fingerboard, one humbucker and two single-coils.*
Similar to STRAT HSS (see later listing), except:
▪ Maple neck, maple fingerboard.
▪ Body black, blue, or red.
▪ One white coverless humbucker (at bridge) and two white six-polepiece pickups.
▪ White plastic pickguard.
Factory Special Run.
031-0702
China

FLOYD ROSE STANDARD STRATOCASTER first version
1992–96 *"Fender" brand logo and "Squier Series" logo on headstock, one humbucker and two single-coils, locking bridge/vibrato system, Foto Flame finish.*
▪ "Squier Series" on headstock with large "Fender" brand logo.
▪ Maple neck, rosewood fingerboard; single-bar string-guide; locking nut.
▪ Body with Foto Flame fake wood finish in blue, red, or natural sunbursts.
▪ One white coverless humbucker (at bridge) and two white six-polepiece pickups.
▪ Two controls (volume, tone) and five-way selector, all on pickguard; output jack in body front.

■ White laminate plastic pickguard.
■ Two-pivot locking bridge/vibrato unit.
Also known as FOTO FLAME FLOYD ROSE STRATOCASTER.
125-5000
Japan

FLOYD ROSE STANDARD STRATOCASTER second version 1994–96 *"Fender" brand logo and "Squier Series" logo on headstock, one humbucker and two single-coils, locking bridge/vibrato system.*
■ "Squier Series" on headstock with large "Fender" brand logo.
■ Maple neck, rosewood or maple fingerboard; single-bar string-guide; locking nut.
■ Body black or white.
■ One white coverless humbucker (at bridge) and two white six-polepiece pickups.
■ Two controls (volume, tone) and five-way selector, all on pickguard: output jack in body front
■ White plastic laminate pickguard.
■ Two-pivot locking bridge/vibrato unit.
113-1100 & 1102
Mexico

FOTO FLAME FLOYD ROSE STRATOCASTER *See earlier listing for FLOYD ROSE STANDARD STRATOCASTER first version.*

JACK DANIELS STRAT HSS 2004–08 *Jack Daniels graphics on black body, one humbucker and two single-coils.*
■ "Affinity Series" on headstock.
■ Maple neck, rosewood fingerboard; truss-rod adjuster at headstock; two string-guides; enlarged (70s-style) headstock.
■ Body black only with Jack Daniels graphics on front.
■ One black coverless humbucker (at bridge) and two black six-polepiece pickups.
■ Three controls (volume, two tone) and five-way selector, all on pickguard; output jack in body front.
■ Grey sparkle plastic pickguard.
■ Six-pivot bridge/vibrato unit.
Part Number not known
China.

OBEY GRAPHIC STRATOCASTER COLLAGE 2006–10 *OBEY Collage graphic on body front.*
■ "Standard Series" on headstock.
■ Maple neck, rosewood fingerboard; 22 frets; truss-rod adjuster at headstock; two string-guides; enlarged (70s-style) headstock.
■ Body black only with OBEY Collage graphic on front.
■ One black coverless humbucker (at bridge) and two black six-polepiece pickups.
■ Three controls (volume, two tone) and five-way selector, all on body; output jack in body front.
■ Two-pivot bridge/vibrato unit.
032-5000
Indonesia

OBEY GRAPHIC STRATOCASTER DISSENT 2006–10 *OBEY Dissent graphic on body front.*
Similar to OBEY GRAPHIC STRATOCASTER COLLAGE (see previous listing), except:
■ Body black only with OBEY Dissent graphic on front.
032-5001
Indonesia

PRO TONE FAT STRAT 1996–98 *Black-face headstock, black pearl pickguard, one black humbucker and two black single-coils, locking bridge/vibrato system, gold-plated hardware.*
■ "Pro Tone Series" on headstock.
■ Maple neck, maple fingerboard; 22 frets; truss-rod adjuster at headstock; single-bar string-guide; locking nut; 'spaghetti'-style "Squier" logo on black-face headstock.
■ Body black only.
■ One black coverless humbucker (at bridge) and two black six-polepiece pickups.
■ Two controls (volume, tone) and five-way selector, all on pickguard; output jack in body front.
■ Black pearl laminate plastic pickguard.
■ Two-pivot locking bridge/vibrato unit.
■ Gold-plated metalwork.
133-3102
Korea

SATIN TRANS FAT STRATOCASTER HSS 2005–07 *Satin-finish body, one black humbucker, two black single-coils, no pickguard.*
Similar to SATIN TRANS FAT STRATOCASTER HH (see earlier listing in Revised Stratocasters: HH), except:
■ Body satin brown, honey, or red.
■ One black coverless humbucker (at bridge) and two black six-polepiece pickups.
■ Three controls (volume, two tone) and five-way selector.
032-1730
Indonesia

SPECIAL STRATOCASTER 1992–93 *"Silver Series" on reverse headstock, one humbucker and two single-coils.*
Limited information available, as follows:
■ "Silver Series" on headstock.
■ Maple neck, rosewood fingerboard; reverse headstock.
■ Body sunburst or colours.
■ One coverless humbucker (at bridge) and two six-polepiece pickups.
■ Two-pivot locking bridge/vibrato unit.
032-8300
Japan

STANDARD FAT STRAT first version 1996–98 *Maple fingerboard, one white humbucker and two white single-coils, white pickguard.*
■ Maple neck, maple fingerboard; truss-rod adjuster at headstock; two string-guides.
■ Body various colours.

- One white coverless humbucker (at bridge) and two white six-polepiece pickups.
- Three controls (volume, two tone) and five-way selector, all on pickguard; output jack in body front.
- White laminate plastic pickguard.
- Six-pivot bridge/vibrato unit.

Also known as CONTEMPORARY STRATOCASTER.
033-1702
Korea

STANDARD FAT STRAT second version 1998–99 *One white humbucker and two white single-coils, white pickguard, one string-guide.*
Similar to STANDARD FAT STRAT first version (see previous listing), except:
- Maple neck, rosewood or maple fingerboard; one string-guide.

013-2200 & 2202
Mexico.

STANDARD FAT STRAT third version 1999–2000 *"Standard Series" on enlarged headstock, one white humbucker and two white single-coils, white pickguard.*
Similar to STANDARD FAT STRAT first version (see earlier listing), except:
- "Standard Series" on headstock.
- Maple neck, rosewood or maple fingerboard; enlarged (70s-style) headstock.
- Body sunburst or colours.
- White laminate plastic pickguard.

032-1700 & 1702
China

STANDARD FAT STRAT fourth version 2000–06 *"Standard Series" on enlarged headstock, 22 frets, one black humbucker and two black single-coils, black pickguard.*
Similar to STANDARD FAT STRAT first version (see earlier listing), except:
- "Standard Series" on headstock.
- Maple neck, rosewood fingerboard only; 22 frets; enlarged (70s-style) headstock, face matches certain body colours.
- Body various colours.
- One black coverless humbucker (at bridge) and two black six-polepiece pickups.
- Black or black laminate plastic pickguard.
- Two-pivot bridge/vibrato unit.

Known as STANDARD STRATOCASTER HSS from 2007 (see later listing).
032-1700
Indonesia

STANDARD FAT STRAT 7 seven-string 2000–02 *Enlarged seven-string headstock, 22 frets, one black humbucker and two black single-coils.*
Similar to STANDARD FAT STRAT fourth version (see previous listing), except:

- "Stratocaster VII" on seven-string headstock.
- One black coverless humbucker (at bridge) and two black seven-polepiece pickups.
- Two-pivot seven-saddle bridge/vibrato unit.

032-1807
Indonesia

STANDARD FAT STRAT FLOYD ROSE 1998–99 *One white humbucker and two white single-coils, two controls, output jack in body front, locking bridge/vibrato system.*
- Maple neck, rosewood or maple fingerboard; truss-rod adjuster at headstock; single-bar string-guide; locking nut.
- Body sunburst or colours.
- One white coverless humbucker (at bridge) and two white six-polepiece pickups.
- Two controls (volume, tone) and five-way selector, all on pickguard; output jack in body front.
- White laminate plastic pickguard.
- Two-pivot locking bridge/vibrato unit.

113-2200 & 2202
Mexico

STANDARD STRATOCASTER HSS 2007–current *"Standard Series" on enlarged headstock, 22 frets, one white humbucker and two white single-coils, white pickguard.*
Similar to STANDARD FAT STRAT fourth version (see earlier listing), except:
- Body black or red.
- One white coverless humbucker (at bridge) and two white six-polepiece pickups.
- White laminate plastic pickguard.

032-1700
Indonesia

STRAT HSS 2001–current *"Strat" and "Affinity Series" on enlarged headstock, one humbucker and two single-coils.*
- "Affinity Series" on headstock.
- Maple neck, rosewood fingerboard; truss-rod adjuster at headstock; two string-guides; enlarged (70s-style) headstock.
- Body various colours.
- One black or white coverless humbucker (at bridge) and two black or white six-polepiece pickups.
- Three controls (volume, two tone) and five-way selector, all on pickguard; output jack in body front.
- Black laminate, grey sparkle, or white plastic pickguard.
- Six-pivot bridge/vibrato unit.

Also known as AFFINITY FAT STRAT, FAT STRAT.
031-0700
China

VINTAGE MODIFIED STRAT HSS 2007–current *One black humbucker and two white six-polepiece pickups.*
- Maple neck, rosewood fingerboard; truss-rod adjuster at headstock; one string-guide.
- Body black or grey.

- One black coverless humbucker (at bridge) and two white six-polepiece pickups.
- Three controls (volume, two tone) and five-way selector, all on pickguard; output jack in body front.
- White laminate plastic pickguard.
- Six-pivot bridge/vibrato unit.

030-1210
India

REVISED STRATOCASTERS: SSS

Three single-coils, or three single-coil-size humbuckers. (For 'unrevised' Stratocasters of this type see the earlier Regular Stratocasters section.)

BLACK & CHROME STANDARD STRATOCASTER

2004–current *Black body, chrome pickguard, three black single-coils.*
- "Standard Series" on headstock.
- Maple neck, rosewood fingerboard; 22 frets; truss-rod adjuster at headstock; two string-guides; black-face enlarged (70s-style) headstock.
- Body black only.
- Three black six-polepiece pickups (bridge pickup angled).
- Three controls (volume, two tone) and five-way selector, all on pickguard; output jack in body front.
- Chrome plastic pickguard.
- Two-pivot bridge/vibrato unit.

032-1603
China

DELUXE FLAME TOP STRATOCASTER 2004–08 *Flame maple body front, white pearl pickguard.*
- "Standard Series" on headstock.
- Maple neck, rosewood fingerboard; 22 frets; truss-rod adjuster at headstock; two string-guides; enlarged (70s-style) headstock.
- Body with flame maple top; sunburst only.
- Three white six-polepiece pickups (bridge pickup angled).
- Three controls (volume, two tone) and five-way selector, all on pickguard; output jack in body front.
- White pearl laminate plastic pickguard.
- Two-pivot bridge/vibrato unit.

Special Edition.
032-1660
Indonesia

DELUXE HOT RAILS STRAT 2007–current *Three black twin-blade pickups.*
- Maple neck, rosewood fingerboard; 22 frets; truss-rod adjuster at headstock; two string-guides; enlarged (70s-style) headstock.
- Body black or white.
- Three black twin-blade pickups (bridge pickup angled).
- Three controls (volume, two tone) and five-way selector, all on pickguard; output jack in body front.
- White laminate plastic pickguard.

- Two-pivot bridge/vibrato unit.

030-0510
Indonesia

DELUXE QUILT TOP STRATOCASTER 2004–08 *Quilt maple body front, white pearl pickguard.*
Similar to DELUXE FLAME TOP STRATOCASTER (see earlier listing), except:
- Body with quilt maple top; sunburst only.

Special Edition.
032-1660
Indonesia

HANK MARVIN STRATOCASTER 1992–93 *Hank Marvin signature on headstock.*
- Maple neck, maple fingerboard; truss-rod adjuster at headstock; one string-guide; Hank Marvin signature on headstock.
- Body red only.
- Three white six-polepiece pickups (bridge pickup angled).
- Three controls (volume, two tone) and five-way selector, all on pickguard; output jack in body front.
- White plastic pickguard.
- Six-pivot bridge/vibrato unit.

032-2002
Japan

HEINEKEN STRATOCASTER 2004–08 *Heineken graphics on front and back of body.*
- Maple neck, rosewood fingerboard; truss-rod adjuster at headstock; two string-guides.
- Body black only with Heineken graphics on front and back.
- Three white six-polepiece pickups (bridge pickup angled).
- Three controls (volume, two tone) and five-way selector, all on pickguard; output jack in body front.
- White laminate plastic pickguard.
- Six-pivot bridge/vibrato unit.

Part Number not known
China

ICEHOUSE STRATOCASTER 2005 *Icehouse graphic on body front.*
- "Standard Series" on headstock.
- Maple neck, rosewood fingerboard; 22 frets; truss-rod adjuster at headstock; two string-guides; enlarged (70s-style) headstock).
- Body black only with (Miller) Icehouse graphics on front.
- Three black six-polepiece pickups (bridge pickup angled).
- Three controls (volume, two tone) and five-way selector, all on body; output jack in body front.
- Six-saddle bridge/tailpiece.

032-2902
Indonesia

JACK DANIELS STRAT 2004–08 *Jack Daniels graphics on black body, three single-coils.*
- "Affinity Series" on headstock.
- Maple neck, rosewood fingerboard; truss-rod adjuster at headstock; two string-guides; enlarged (70s-style) headstock.
- Body black only with Jack Daniels graphics on front or front and back (two different designs).
- Three white six-polepiece pickups (bridge pickup angled).
- Three controls (volume, two tone) and five-way selector, all on pickguard; jack socket in body front.
- White plastic pickguard.
- Six-pivot bridge/vibrato unit.

Part Number not known
China.

MILLER GENUINE DRAFT STRATOCASTER 2004–08 *Miller Genuine Draft graphic on body front.*
- "Standard Series" on headstock.
- Maple neck, rosewood fingerboard; 22 frets; truss-rod adjuster at headstock; two string-guides; enlarged (70s-style) headstock.
- Body black only with Miller Lite graphic on front.
- Three black six-polepiece pickups (bridge pickup angled).
- Three controls (volume, two tone) and five-way selector, all on body; output jack in body front.
- Six-saddle bridge/tailpiece.

032-2905
Indonesia

MILLER LITE STRATOCASTER 2004–08 *Miller Lite graphic on body front.*
- "Standard Series" on headstock.
- Maple neck, rosewood fingerboard; 22 frets; truss-rod adjuster at headstock; two string-guides; enlarged (70s-style) headstock.
- Body silver only with Miller Lite graphic on front.
- Three white six-polepiece pickups (bridge pickup angled).
- Three controls (volume, two tone) and five-way selector, all on body; output jack in body front.
- Six-saddle bridge/tailpiece.

032-2900
Indonesia

O-LARN SIGNATURE STRATOCASTER 2006–current *O-Larn signature on enlarged headstock.*
- Maple neck, rosewood fingerboard; 22 frets; truss-rod adjuster at headstock; two string-guides; O-Larn signature on enlarged (70s-style) headstock.
- Body sunburst or colours.
- Three black twin-blade pickups (bridge pickup angled).
- One control (volume) and five-way selector, both on pickguard; output jack in body front.
- White laminate plastic pickguard.
- Two-pivot bridge/vibrato unit.

Sold in Thailand only.
032-7800
China

SHAM KAMIKAZE STRATOCASTER 2009–current *Sham Kamikaze signature on reverse enlarged headstock.*
- Maple neck, maple fingerboard; truss-rod adjuster at headstock; one string-guide; Sham Kamikaze signature on reverse enlarged (70s-style) headstock.
- Body black or white.
- Three white six-polepiece pickups (bridge pickup reverse-angled).
- Three controls (volume, two tone) and five-way selector, all on pickguard; output jack in body front.
- White plastic pickguard.
- Six-pivot bridge/vibrato unit.

Sold in Malaysia only.
030-1050
China

SIMON NEIL STRATOCASTER 2009–current *Simon Neil signature on headstock back, Biffy Clyro band logo on headstock front.*
- Maple neck, rosewood fingerboard; truss-rod adjuster at headstock; one string-guide; Simon Neil signature on headstock back, Biffy Clyro band logo on headstock front.
- Body red only.
- Three white six-polepiece pickups (bridge pickup angled).
- Three controls (volume, two tone) and five-way selector.
- White laminate plastic pickguard.
- Six-pivot bridge/vibrato unit.

Sold in Europe only.
030-1028
China

STANDARD STRATOCASTER 1987–88 *String clamp on headstock, no string-guides, three white single-coils, two-pivot bridge/vibrato unit with fine tuners.*
- Maple neck, rosewood or maple fingerboard; truss-rod adjuster at body; no string-guides; string clamp on headstock.
- Body black, red, or white.
- Three white six-polepiece pickups (bridge pickup angled).
- Three controls (volume, two tone) and five-way selector, all on pickguard; output jack in body front.
- White or white laminate plastic pickguard.
- Two-pivot bridge/vibrato unit with fine tuners.

027-8800 & 8802
Japan

WAYNE'S WORLD STRATOCASTER first version 1992–93 *"Wayne's World" on neck-plate.*
- Maple neck, rosewood fingerboard; truss-rod adjuster at headstock; one string-guide; "Wayne's World" on neck-plate.
- Body white only.
- Three white six-polepiece pickups (bridge pickup angled).
- Three controls (volume, two tone) and five-way selector, all on pickguard; output jack in body front.
- White laminate plastic pickguard.
- Six-pivot bridge/vibrato unit.

032-1000
Japan

WAYNE'S WORLD STRATOCASTER second version 1993
Limited information available, as follows:
- Maple neck, rosewood or maple fingerboard.
- Body black or white.
- Six-pivot bridge/vibrato unit.
032-1100 & 032-1102
Japan

WAYNE'S WORLD STRATOCASTER FLOYD ROSE 1993
Limited information available, as follows:
- Maple neck, rosewood or maple fingerboard.
- Body black or white.
- Two-pivot locking bridge/vibrato unit.
132-1100 & 132-1102
Japan

REGULAR TELECASTERS

Since the Squier brand was introduced in 1982, Fender has produced many versions of what we define as the 'Regular' Squier Telecaster. All examples have "Telecaster" or "Tele" on the headstock. Also on the headstock is information that can provide pointers to a specific series, to the guitar's country of origin, and to its production date, as explained on page 126 under The Headstock: Instant Information. All Telecasters have Body Shape 2 – see page 139.

'REGULAR' TELECASTER 1982–current
- Maple neck, rosewood or maple fingerboard; 21 or 22 frets; truss-rod adjuster at body or at headstock; one or two string-guides; "Telecaster" or "Tele" on headstock; headstock face natural or colour.
- Solid slab (not contoured) single-cutaway body; sunburst or colours.
- One plain metal-cover pickup (at neck) and one six-polepiece pickup (angled in bridge-plate).
- Two controls (volume, tone) and three-way selector, all on metal plate adjoining pickguard; side-mounted output jack.
- Laminate or single-layer plastic pickguard.
- Flat or raised-sides bridge-plate with three or six bridge saddles, through-body or top-loaded stringing.
- Nickel, chrome, gold, or black-plated metalwork.

* Some 'Regular' Telecasters have a series name on the headstock:
"Affinity Series" (1997–current)
"California Series" (2003–current)
"Silver Series" (1992–94)
"Squier Series" with large Fender logo (1982 Japan, 1992–94 Korea, 1994–96 Mexico)
"Standard Series" (1999–current)
* Some 'Regular' Telecasters are known by a series name that is not on the guitar but is used in catalogues, ads, pricelists, etc. These series include:
Classic Vibe (2008–current)
Popular (UK; simply 'Squier Telecaster' US), aka 'SQ' (1983–84)
Standard (1985–99)
Tradition/Traditional (1996)
'52 Telecaster (1982–84)
China, Indonesia, Japan, Korea, Mexico

REVISED TELECASTERS

Listed next are the models we regard as Fender's altered and adapted versions of the 'Regular' Squier Telecaster (for which see the earlier *Regular Telecasters* section). These 'Revised' Telecasters incorporate significant visible changes to cosmetics, construction, and/or components. For ease of reference we've divided them into sections based on pickup configurations. They are arranged in the following order:

H   One humbucker (at bridge).
HH   Two humbuckers.
HS   One humbucker (at bridge) and one single-coil (at neck).
HSH   Two humbuckers and one single-coil (in centre).
HSS   One humbucker (at bridge) and two single-coils.
SH   One single-coil (at bridge) and one humbucker (at neck).
SS   Two single-coils.
SSH   Two single-coils and one humbucker (at neck).

REVISED TELECASTERS: H
One humbucker (at bridge).

AVRIL LAVIGNE TELECASTER 2007–current *Avril Lavigne signature on headstock.*
- Maple neck, rosewood fingerboard, no markers except star at 5th fret; 22 frets; truss-rod adjuster at headstock; two string-guides; Avril Lavigne signature on headstock.
- Solid slab single-cutaway body; black only.
- One black coverless humbucker (at bridge).
- One control (volume), three-way selector, and output jack, all on metal plate adjoining pickguard.
- Black/white checkerboard-pattern pickguard.
- Six-saddle small bridge with through-body stringing.
030-1010
Indonesia

DERYCK WHIBLEY TELECASTER 2007–current *"Deryck" on Stratocaster-style enlarged headstock, red cross graphics on body and pickguard.*
- Maple neck, maple fingerboard; truss-rod adjuster at headstock; two string-guides; "Deryck" on Stratocaster-style enlarged (70s-style) headstock.
- Solid slab single-cutaway body; black or white with red cross graphic on front.
- One metal-cover humbucker (at bridge).
- Two controls (volume, tone) on pickguard; side-mounted output jack.
- Black laminate plastic pickguard with red cross graphic.

■ Six-saddle small bridge with through-body stringing.
030-1000
Indonesia

REVISED TELECASTERS: HH
Two humbuckers.

CHAMBERED TELE HH 2005–07 *Glued-in neck, slim block markers, single-cutaway bound body, two metal-cover humbuckers.*
■ Mahogany glued-in neck, bound rosewood fingerboard, slim block markers; 22 frets; truss-rod adjuster at headstock; two string-guides; neck and headstock face match body colour.
■ Semi-solid slab single-cutaway bound body; various colours.
■ Two metal-cover humbuckers.
■ Four controls (two volume, two tone) and three-way selector, all on body; side-mounted output jack.
■ Six-saddle slim bridge, separate tailpiece.
034-0200
Korea

DOUBLE FAT TELECASTER DELUXE 2001–03 *Glued-in neck, carved-front body, two black humbuckers.*
■ Mahogany glued-in neck, rosewood fingerboard; 22 frets; truss-rod adjuster at headstock; two string-guides; neck and headstock face match body colour.
■ Solid carved-front single-cutaway body; black, blue, or red.
■ Two black coverless humbuckers.
■ Two controls (volume, tone) and three-way selector, all on body; side-mounted output jack.
■ Six-saddle small bridge with through-body stringing.
■ Black-plated metalwork.
032-2300
Korea

J5 TELECASTER 2009–current *Bound black body, two black humbuckers with one in bridge-plate, polished metal pickguard.*
■ Maple neck, rosewood fingerboard; 22 frets; truss-rod adjuster at headstock; one string-guide; black-face headstock.
■ Solid slab single-cutaway bound body; black only.
■ Two black coverless humbuckers (one in bridge-plate).
■ Two controls (two volume) on metal plate adjacent to pickguard; three-way selector on body; side-mounted output jack.
■ Polished metal pickguard.
■ Six-saddle flat bridge with through-body stringing.
030-1005
China

TELE HH FSR 2011 *"Tele" on headstock, two black humbuckers, black pickguard.*
■ Maple neck, rosewood fingerboard; 22 frets; truss-rod adjuster at headstock; two string-guides.
■ Solid slab single-cutaway body; sunburst, black, or red.
■ Two black coverless humbuckers.
■ Two controls (volume, tone) and three-way selector, all on metal plate; side-mounted output jack.

■ Black laminate plastic pickguard.
■ Six-saddle small bridge/tailpiece.
Factory Special Run.
031-0035
China

TELECASTER CUSTOM *See later listing for VINTAGE MODIFIED TELECASTER CUSTOM in Revised Telecasters: HH.*

THINLINE TELE HH 2005–07 *Glued-in neck, bound body with f-hole, two black humbuckers.*
■ "Standard Series" on headstock.
■ Maple glued-in neck, rosewood fingerboard; 22 frets; truss-rod adjuster at headstock; two string-guides; neck and headstock face match body colour.
■ Semi-solid slab single-cutaway bound body with f-hole; black, natural, or red.
■ Two black coverless humbuckers.
■ Four controls (two volume, two tone) and three-way selector, all on body; side-mounted output jack.
■ Six-saddle small bridge with through-body stringing.
034-0100
China

VINTAGE MODIFIED TELECASTER CUSTOM 2003–current *"Telecaster Custom" on headstock, two metal-cover humbuckers.*
■ Maple neck, maple fingerboard; 22 frets; truss-rod adjuster at headstock; two string-guides.
■ Solid slab single-cutaway body; black only.
■ Two metal-cover humbuckers.
■ Four controls (two volume, two tone) and three-way selector, all on pickguard; side-mounted output jack.
■ Black laminate plastic pickguard.
■ Six-saddle small bridge with through-body stringing.
032-7502
China

REVISED TELECASTERS: HS
One humbucker (at bridge) and one single-coil (at neck).

OBEY GRAPHIC TELECASTER COLLAGE 2006–10 *OBEY Collage graphic on body front.*
■ "Standard Series" on headstock.
■ Maple neck, rosewood fingerboard; 22 frets; truss-rod adjuster at headstock; two string-guides.
■ Solid slab single-cutaway body; black only with OBEY Collage graphic on front.
■ One black coverless humbucker (at bridge) and one black six-polepiece pickup (at neck).
■ Two controls (volume, tone) and three-way selector, all on metal plate; side-mounted output jack.
■ Six-saddle small bridge with through-body stringing.
032-5002
Indonesia

- Six-saddle flat bridge with through-body stringing.
032-1300
Indonesia

STANDARD TELECASTER SH WITH BIGSBY FSR 2010
Bigsby vibrato tailpiece, red body.
- "Standard Series" on headstock.
- Maple neck, rosewood fingerboard; 22 frets; truss-rod adjuster at headstock; two string-guides.
- Solid slab single-cutaway body; red only.
- One black six-polepiece pickup (angled in bridge-plate) and one metal-cover humbucker (at neck).
- Two controls (volume, tone) and three-way selector, all on metal plate adjoining pickguard; side-mounted jack socket.
- Eight-screw white laminate plastic pickguard.
- Six-saddle bridge, Bigsby vibrato tailpiece.
Factory Special Run.
Part Number not known
Indonesia

VINTAGE MODIFIED TELE SH 2007–current *One black single-coil and one black/cream humbucker, reversed control plate.*
- Maple neck, maple fingerboard; truss-rod adjuster at headstock; two string-guides.
- Solid slab single-cutaway body; black or red.
- One black six-polepiece pickup (angled in bridge-plate) and one black/white coverless humbucker (at neck).
- Two controls (volume, tone) and three-way selector, all on reversed metal plate adjoining pickguard; side-mounted output jack.
- White laminate plastic pickguard.
- Six-saddle raised-sides bridge with through-body stringing.
030-1235
India

REVISED TELECASTERS: SS
Two single-coils.

BLACK & CHROME TELECASTER 2004–current *Black body, chrome pickguard.*
- "Standard Series" on headstock.
- Maple neck, rosewood fingerboard; 22 frets; truss-rod adjuster at headstock; two string-guides; black-face headstock.
- Solid slab single-cutaway body; black only.
- One black six-polepiece pickup (angled in bridge-plate) and one plain metal-cover pickup (at neck).
- Two controls (volume, tone) and three-way selector, all on pickguard; side-mounted output jack.
- Chrome plastic pickguard.
- Six-saddle flat bridge with through-body stringing.
032-1203
Indonesia

CLASSIC VIBE TELECASTER CUSTOM 2010–current
"Telecaster Custom" on headstock, bound body, two single-coils.

- Maple neck, rosewood fingerboard; truss-rod adjuster at headstock; one string-guide.
- Solid slab single-cutaway bound body; sunburst only.
- One black six-polepiece pickup (angled in bridge-plate) and one plain metal-cover pickup (at neck).
- Two controls (volume, tone) and three-way selector, all on metal plate adjoining pickguard; side-mounted output jack.
- White laminate plastic pickguard.
- Three-saddle raised-sides bridge with through-body stringing.
030-3030
China

CLASSIC VIBE TELECASTER THINLINE 2010–current *Body with f-hole, two single-coils, three-saddle bridge.*
- Maple neck, maple fingerboard; truss-rod adjuster at headstock; one string-guide.
- Semi-solid slab single-cutaway body with f-hole; brown only.
- One black six-polepiece pickup (angled in bridge-plate) and one plain metal-cover pickup (at neck).
- Two controls (volume, tone) and three-way selector, all on pickguard; side-mounted output jack.
- White pearl laminate plastic pickguard.
- Three-saddle raised-sides bridge with through-body stringing.
030-3035
China

PRO TONE THINLINE TELE 1996–98 *'Spaghetti'-style "Squier" logo, f-hole body, white pearl pickguard.*
- "Pro Tone Series" on headstock.
- Maple neck, maple fingerboard; truss-rod adjuster at headstock; one string-guide; 'spaghetti'-style "Squier" logo.
- Semi-solid slab single-cutaway bound body, f-hole; red only.
- One black six-polepiece pickup (angled in bridge-plate) and one plain metal-cover pickup (at neck).
- Two controls (volume, tone) and three-way selector.
- White pearl laminate plastic pickguard.
- Six-saddle flat bridge with through-body stringing.
- Gold-plated hardware.
033-3802
Korea

ROLLING ROCK TELECASTER 2008 *Rolling Rock graphic on body front.*
- "Standard Series" on headstock.
- Maple neck, rosewood fingerboard; 22 frets; truss-rod adjuster at headstock; two string-guides.
- Solid slab single-cutaway body; green only with Rolling Rock graphic on front (three different designs).
- One black six-polepiece pickup (angled in bridge-plate) and one plain metal-cover pickup (at neck).
- Two controls (volume, tone) and three-way selector, all on metal plate adjoining pickguard; side-mounted output jack.
- White laminate plastic pickguard.
- Six-saddle flat bridge with through-body stringing.
032-2201
Indonesia

TELECASTER CUSTOM *See earlier listing for CLASSIC VIBE TELECASTER CUSTOM or next listing for VINTAGE MODIFIED TELECASTER CUSTOM II.*

VINTAGE MODIFIED TELECASTER CUSTOM II

2004–current *"Telecaster Custom" on headstock, two large black single-coils.*
- Maple neck, maple fingerboard; 22 frets; truss-rod adjuster at headstock; two string-guides.
- Solid slab single-cutaway body; black or blonde.
- Two large black six-polepiece pickups.
- Four controls (two volume, two tone) and three-way selector, all on pickguard; side-mounted output jack.
- Black laminate plastic pickguard.
- Six-saddle small bridge with through-body stringing.
032-7602
China

VINTAGE MODIFIED TELECASTER THINLINE 2007–current

Body with f-hole, two single-coils, six-saddle bridge.
- Maple neck, rosewood fingerboard; 24.75-inch scale, 22 frets; truss-rod adjuster at headstock; one string-guide.
- Semi-solid slab single-cutaway body with f-hole; black or gold.
- One black six-polepiece pickup (angled in bridge-plate) and one plain metal-cover pickup (at neck).

- Two controls (volume, tone) and three-way selector, all on pickguard; side-mounted output jack.
- White laminate plastic pickguard.
- Six-saddle raised-sides bridge with through-body stringing.
030-1240
China

REVISED TELECASTERS: SSH

Two single-coils and one humbucker (at neck).

VINTAGE MODIFIED TELE SSH 2007–current *One metal-cover mini-humbucker, one white and one black six-polepiece pickup, reversed control plate.*
Similar to VINTAGE MODIFIED TELE SH (see earlier listing in Revised Telecasters: SH), except:
- Body black or white.
- One black six-polepiece pickup (angled in bridge-plate), one white six-polepiece pickup (centre), and one plain-top metal-cover mini-humbucker (at neck).
- Two controls (volume, tone) and five-way selector, all on reversed metal plate adjoining pickguard.
- Black laminate or white laminate plastic pickguard.
030-1230
India

OTHER MODELS

These are listed on the pages that follow in the alphabetical order of the model name. At the head of each instrument entry, after the model name is a body shape reference number (in brackets). This refers to the relevant numbered silhouette shown in the Body Shape Key below. These 20 body shapes will help you to identify particular Squier models within the following Other Models section.

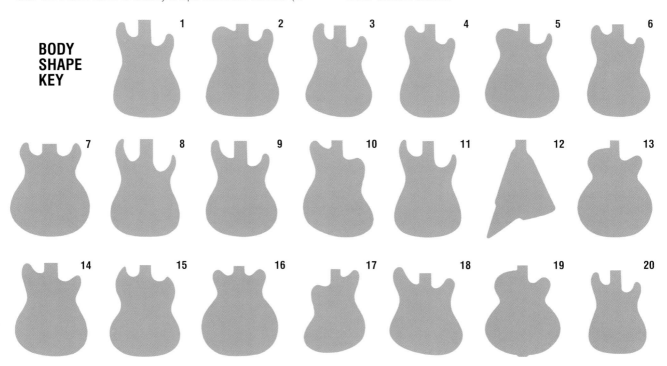

BODY SHAPE KEY

BLACKOUT SHOWMASTER HS *See later listing for SHOWMASTER HS BLACKOUT.*

BULLET first version (1) 1995–96 *"Bullet" on Stratocaster-style headstock, 22 frets, three single-coils, six-pivot bridge/vibrato unit.*
- Maple neck, rosewood fingerboard; 22 frets; truss-rod adjuster at headstock; one string-guide.
- Body black, red, or white.
- Three white six-polepiece pickups (bridge pickup angled).
- Three controls (volume, two tone) and five-way selector, all on pickguard; output jack in body front.
- White plastic pickguard.
- Six-pivot bridge/vibrato unit.
033-0600
Korea

BULLET second version (1) 2000–07 *"Bullet" on Stratocaster-style headstock, three single-coils, six-saddle bridge/tailpiece.*
- Maple neck, rosewood fingerboard; truss-rod adjuster at headstock; two string-guides.
- Body black, blue, or red.
- Three white six-polepiece pickups (bridge pickup angled).
- Three controls (volume, two tone) and five-way selector, all on pickguard; output jack in body front.
- White plastic pickguard.
- Six-saddle small bridge/tailpiece.
031-0000
Indonesia

BULLET third version (1) 2005–06 *"Bullet" on Stratocaster-style headstock, three single-coils, six-pivot bridge/vibrato unit.*
- Maple neck, maple fingerboard; truss-rod adjuster at headstock; two string-guides.
- Body black or blue.
- Three white six-polepiece pickups (bridge pickup angled).
- Three controls (volume, two tone) and five-way selector, all on pickguard; output jack in body front.
- White plastic pickguard.
- Six-pivot bridge/vibrato unit.
033-1100
China

BULLET DELUXE (1) 2003–04 *"Bullet" on Stratocaster-style headstock, one white humbucker, one control, six-saddle bridge with through-body stringing.*
- Maple neck, rosewood fingerboard; truss-rod adjuster at headstock; two string-guides.
- Body black or green.
- One white coverless humbucker at bridge.
- One control (volume) on pickguard.
- Black or white plastic pickguard.
- Six-saddle small bridge with through-body stringing.
031-8201
China

BULLET H-2 (3) 1983–86 *"Bullet" on Telecaster-style headstock, two white plain-top humbuckers.*
- Maple neck, maple fingerboard; truss-rod adjuster at body; one string-guide.
- Solid slab offset-double-cutaway body; sunburst or colours.
- Two white plain-top humbuckers.
- Two controls (volume, tone), three-way selector, two pushbutton coil-switches, and output jack, all on pickguard.
- White laminate plastic pickguard.
- Six-saddle small bridge with through-body stringing.
026-5595
Japan

BULLET HH HT FSR (1) 2010 *"Bullet" on Stratocaster-style headstock, two coverless humbuckers.*
- Maple neck, rosewood fingerboard; truss-rod adjuster at headstock; two string-guides.
- Body black, red, or white.
- Two black or white coverless humbuckers.
- Three controls (volume, two tone) and three-way selector.
- Black laminate or white laminate plastic pickguard.
- Six-saddle bridge/tailpiece.
Factory Special Run.
031-0025
Indonesia

BULLET HH WITH TREMOLO FSR (1) 2010–11 *"Bullet" on Strat-style headstock, two black humbuckers, black-plated metalwork.*
- Maple neck, rosewood fingerboard; truss-rod adjuster at headstock; two string-guides.
- Body sunburst or colours.
- Two black coverless humbuckers.
- Three controls (volume, two tone) and three-way selector, all on pickguard; output jack in body front.
- Black laminate plastic pickguard.
- Six-pivot bridge/vibrato unit.
- Black-plated metalwork.
Factory Special Run.
031-0020
China

BULLET S-3 (3) 1983–86 *"Bullet" on Telecaster-style headstock, three white plain-top single-coils.*
Similar to BULLET H-2 (see earlier listing), except:
- Three white plain-top pickups (bridge pickup angled).
- Two controls (volume, tone), five-way selector, and output jack, all on pickguard.
026-5586
Japan

BULLET S-3T first version (3) 1983–85 *"Bullet" on Tele-style headstock, three white single-coils, six-pivot bridge/vibrato unit.*
Similar to BULLET S-3 (see previous listing), except:
- Six-pivot bridge/vibrato unit.
026-5590
Japan

BULLET S-3T second version (3) 1986–87 *"Bullet" on Telecaster-style headstock, three white single-coils, two-pivot bridge/vibrato unit.*
Similar to BULLET S-3 (see earlier listing), except:
- Body sunburst or black.
- Two-pivot bridge/vibrato unit.
027-7002
Japan

BULLET S-3T third version (3) 1987–88 *"Bullet" on Stratocaster-style headstock, three white single-coils, two-pivot bridge/vibrato unit.*
Similar to BULLET S-3 (see earlier listing), except:
- Maple neck, rosewood fingerboard; truss-rod adjuster at headstock.
- Body black or red.
- Two-pivot bridge/vibrato unit.
027-8400
Japan, Korea

BULLET SPECIAL (1) 2002–07 *"Bullet" on Stratocaster-style headstock, one humbucker, one control.*
Similar to BULLET second version (see earlier listing), except:
- Body sunburst or colours.
- One black or white coverless humbucker (at bridge).
- One control (volume) on pickguard.
- Black plastic pickguard.
- Black or chrome-plated metalwork.
032-0000
Indonesia

BULLET STRAT WITH TREMOLO (1) 2007–current *"Bullet Strat" on headstock, three white single-coils, white pickguard.*
- Maple neck, rosewood fingerboard; truss-rod adjuster at headstock; two string-guides.
- Body sunburst or colours.
- Three white six-polepiece pickups (bridge pickup angled).
- Three controls (volume, two tone) and five-way selector, all on pickguard; output jack in body front.
- White plastic pickguard.
- Six-pivot bridge/vibrato unit.
031-0001
China

BULLET STRAT HSS WITH TREMOLO (1) 2010–current *"Bullet Strat" on headstock, one white humbucker and two white single-coils, white pickguard.*
- Maple neck, rosewood fingerboard; truss-rod adjuster at headstock; two string-guides.
- Body sunburst, black, or white.
- One white coverless humbucker (at bridge) and two white six-polepiece pickups.
- Three controls (volume, two tone) and five-way selector, all on pickguard; output jack in body front.

- White plastic pickguard.
- Six-pivot bridge/vibrato unit.
031-0005
China

CLASSIC VIBE DUO-SONIC 50s (4) 2008–current *"Duo-Sonic" on headstock, 21 frets, gold pickguard.*
- Maple neck, maple fingerboard; 24-inch scale; truss-rod adjuster at headstock; plastic tuner buttons; one string-guide.
- Solid semi-contoured offset-double-cutaway body; gold only.
- Two cream plain-top pickups (neck pickup angled).
- Two controls (volume, tone), three-way selector, and output jack, all on pickguard.
- Anodised gold metal pickguard.
- Three-saddle small bridge/tailpiece.
030-3050
China

CONTEMPORARY BULLET HST first version (5) 1985–86 *"Bullet" on Stratocaster-style headstock, one black humbucker and two black single-coils, no pickguard, single-cutaway body.*
- Maple neck, maple fingerboard; truss-rod adjuster at body; one string-guide.
- Solid slab single-cutaway body; black or white.
- One black coverless humbucker (at bridge) and two black six-polepiece pickups.
- Two controls (volume, tone) and five-way selector, all on body; side-mounted output jack.
- Two-pivot bridge/vibrato unit.
Part Number not known
Japan

CONTEMPORARY BULLET HST second version (3) 1986–87 *"Bullet" on Telecaster-style headstock, one white plain-top humbucker and two plain-top white single-coils, white pickguard.*
- Maple neck, maple fingerboard; truss-rod adjuster at body; one string-guide.
- Solid offset-double-cutaway body; black or white.
- One white plain-top humbucker at bridge and two white plain-top single-coil pickups.
- Two controls (volume, tone), five-way selector, and output jack, all on pickguard.
- White laminate plastic pickguard.
- Two-pivot bridge/vibrato unit.
027-7202
Japan

CONTEMPORARY BULLET HST third version (3) 1987–88 *"Bullet" on Stratocaster-style headstock, one black humbucker and two black single-coils, no pickguard.*
- Maple neck, rosewood fingerboard; truss-rod adjuster at headstock; one string-guide.
- Solid slab offset-double-cutaway body; black or white.
- One black coverless humbucker (at bridge) and two black six-polepiece pickups.

- Two controls (volume, tone) and five-way selector, all on body; side-mounted output jack.
- Two-pivot bridge/vibrato unit.

027-8500

Japan, Korea

CYCLONE (6) 2003–07 *"Cyclone" on headstock.*
- Maple neck, rosewood fingerboard; 24.75-inch scale, 22 frets; truss-rod adjuster at headstock; one string-guide.
- Solid contoured offset-waist offset-double-cutaway body; various colours.
- One white coverless humbucker (at bridge) and one white six-polepiece pickup (angled at neck).
- Two controls (volume, tone) and output jack, all on metal plate adjoining pickguard; three-way selector on pickguard.
- White pearl laminate plastic pickguard.
- Six-pivot bridge/vibrato unit.

032-0500

Indonesia

DUO-SONIC (6) 1998–99 *"Duo-Sonic" on headstock, 20 frets, white pickguard.*
- "Affinity Series" on headstock.
- Maple neck, maple fingerboard; 22.7-inch scale, 20 frets; truss-rod adjuster at headstock; one string-guide.
- Solid slab offset-waist offset-double-cutaway body; various colours.
- Two white six-polepiece pickups (both angled).
- Two controls (volume, tone), three-way selector, and output jack, all on pickguard.
- White plastic pickguard.
- Three-saddle small bridge/tailpiece.

See also CLASSIC VIBE DUO SONIC in earlier listing.

033-0702

China

ESPRIT (7) 2005–07 *"Esprit" on three-tuners-per-side headstock.*
- Mahogany glued-in neck, bound rosewood fingerboard, slim block markers; 24.75-inch scale, 22 frets; truss-rod adjuster at headstock; three-tuners-per-side black-face headstock; neck matches body colour.
- Semi-solid twin-cutaway bound body; sunburst, black, or red.
- Two metal-cover humbuckers.
- Four controls (two volume, two tone) and three-way selector, all on body; side-mounted output jack.
- Six-saddle slim bridge, separate slim tailpiece.

Master Series.

034-3000

Korea

FR-211 (8) 1992–94 *Large underlined "Squier" logo on angular black-face headstock, one black humbucker and two black single-coils on black pickguard, locking bridge/vibrato system.*
- Maple neck, rosewood fingerboard; 22 frets; truss-rod adjuster at headstock; single-bar string-guide; locking nut; large underlined "Squier" logo on angular black-face headstock.

- Solid slim-horned offset-double-cutaway body; various colours.
- One black coverless humbucker (at bridge) and two black six-polepiece pickups.
- Two controls (volume, tone) and five-way selector, all on pickguard; side-mounted output jack.
- Black laminate plastic pickguard.
- Two-pivot locking bridge/vibrato unit.
- Black-plated metalwork.

133-8100

Korea

FR-211ST (1) 1992–94 *Black-face Stratocaster-style headstock, one black humbucker and two black single-coils, black pickguard, locking bridge/vibrato system.*
- Maple neck, rosewood fingerboard; 22 frets; truss-rod adjuster at headstock; single-bar string-guide; locking nut; black-face Stratocaster-style headstock.
- Body various colours.
- One black coverless humbucker (at bridge) and two black six-polepiece pickups.
- Two controls (volume, tone) and five-way selector, all on pickguard; output jack in body front.
- 11-screw black laminate plastic pickguard.
- Two-pivot locking bridge/vibrato unit.
- Black-plated metalwork.

133-8300

Korea

FR-212 (8) 1992–94 *Large underlined Squier logo on black-face angular reverse headstock, two black humbuckers and one black single-coil, locking bridge/vibrato system.*

Similar to FR-211 (see earlier listing), except:
- Black-face angular reverse headstock.
- Two black coverless humbuckers and one black six-polepiece pickup (in centre).
- Two controls (volume, tone) and five-way selector, all on body.
- No pickguard.

133-8000

Korea

HELLO KITTY MINI (20) 2006–09 *"Mini" on headstock, Hello Kitty logo graphic on body.*

Similar to MINI (see later listing), except:
- Body black or pink with Hello Kitty logo graphic.

033-5101

Indonesia

H.M. I (9) 1989–93 *Large underlined "Squier" logo on angular black-face headstock, one black humbucker and two black single-coils, two-pivot bridge/vibrato unit.*
- Maple neck, rosewood fingerboard; 22 frets; truss-rod adjuster at headstock; large underlined "Squier" logo on angular black-face headstock.
- Solid slim-horned offset-double-cutaway body; various colours.
- One black coverless humbucker (at bridge) and two black six-polepiece pickups.

■ Two controls (volume, tone) and five-way selector, all on body; side-mounted output jack.
■ Two-pivot bridge/vibrato unit.
■ Black-plated metalwork.
033-1300 & 133-1300
Korea

H.M. II (9) 1989–93 *Large underlined "Squier" logo on angular black-face headstock, one black humbucker and two black single-coils, locking bridge/vibrato system.*
Similar to H.M. I (see previous listing), except:
■ Single-bar string-guide; locking nut.
■ Two-pivot locking bridge/vibrato unit.
033-1200 & 133-1200
Korea

H.M. III (9) 1989–93 *Large underlined "Squier" logo on angular black-face headstock, two black humbuckers and one black single-coil, locking bridge/vibrato system.*
Similar to H.M. I (see earlier listing), except:
■ Single-bar string-guide; locking nut.
■ Two black coverless humbuckers and one black six-polepiece pickup (in centre).
■ Two-pivot locking bridge/vibrato unit.
033-1100 & 133-1100
Korea

H.M. IV (9) 1990–93 *Large underlined "Squier" logo on angular black-face headstock, two black humbuckers and one black single-coil, locking bridge/vibrato system, through-neck.*
Similar to H.M. I (see earlier listing), except:
■ Through-neck; single-bar string-guide; locking nut.
■ Two black coverless humbuckers and one black six-polepiece pickup (in centre).
■ Two-pivot locking bridge/vibrato unit.
033-2200 & 133-2200
Korea

H.M. V (9) 1990–93 *Large underlined "Squier" logo on angular black-face headstock, two black humbuckers and one black single-coil, locking bridge/vibrato system, figured body top.*
Similar to H.M. I (see earlier listing), except:
■ Through-neck; single-bar string-guide; locking nut.
■ Body with figured top.
■ Two black coverless humbuckers and one black six-polepiece pickup (in centre).
■ Two-pivot locking bridge/vibrato unit.
033-2100 & 133-2100
Korea

J MASCIS JAZZMASTER (10) 2011–current *J Mascis signature on headstock.*
■ Maple neck, rosewood fingerboard; truss-rod adjuster at headstock; one string-guide; J Mascis signature on headstock.
■ Solid contoured offset-waist body; white only.
■ Two large white six-polepiece pickups.

■ Two controls (volume, tone), two rollers (volume, tone), three-way selector, slide switch, and output jack, all on pickguard.
■ Anodised gold metal pickguard.
■ Six-saddle slim bridge, vibrato tailpiece.
030-1060
Indonesia

JACK DANIELS SHOWMASTER *See later listing for SHOWMASTER HSS NLT JACK DANIELS.*

JAGMASTER first version (10) 1997–98 *"Jagmaster" on headstock, 24-inch scale, 22 frets, two humbuckers.*
■ "Vista Series" on headstock.
■ Maple neck, rosewood fingerboard; 24-inch scale, 22 frets; truss-rod adjuster at body; one string-guide.
■ Solid contoured offset-waist body; sunburst or colours.
■ Two white coverless humbuckers.
■ Two controls (volume, tone), three-way selector, and output jack, all on pickguard.
■ Brown shell laminate plastic pickguard.
■ Six-pivot bridge/vibrato unit.
027-1600
Japan

JAGMASTER second version (10) 2000–04 *"Jagmaster" on headstock, 25.5-inch scale, 21 or 22 frets, two humbuckers.*
Similar to JAGMASTER first version (see previous listing), except:
■ 25.5-inch scale, 21 or 22 frets; truss-rod adjuster at headstock; two string-guides; enlarged (70s-style) headstock.
■ Body black, red, or silver.
■ Two black or white coverless humbuckers.
■ Black or black laminate plastic pickguard.
032-0700
China

JAGMASTER third version (10) 2005–current *"Jagmaster" on headstock, 24-inch scale, 21 frets, two humbuckers.*
Similar to JAGMASTER first version (see earlier listing), except:
■ "Standard Series" on headstock.
■ 21 frets; truss-rod adjuster at headstock; two string-guides; enlarged (70s-style) headstock.
■ Body sunburst or black.
■ Two black or white coverless humbuckers.
■ Brown shell laminate or white laminate plastic pickguard.
032-0700
China

JAGUAR *See later listing for VINTAGE MODIFIED JAGUAR HH.*

JASON ELLIS SIGNATURE SHOWMASTER *See later listing for SHOWMASTER JASON ELLIS SIGNATURE.*

JAZZMASTER *See earlier listing for J MASCIS JAZZMASTER and later listing for VINTAGE MODIFIED JAZZMASTER.*

KATANA (12) 1985–87 *"Katana" on headstock, wedge-shape body.*
- Maple neck, rosewood fingerboard; 24.75-inch scale; truss-rod adjuster at body; two string-guides; arrowhead-shape headstock.
- Solid bevelled-edge wedge-shape body; black or white.
- One black coverless humbucker (at bridge).
- One control (volume) on body; side-mounted output jack.
- Six-pivot bridge/vibrato unit.

027-5600
Japan

M-50 (13) 2002–05 *Three-tuners-per-side headstock, bolt-on neck, single-cutaway body, two black humbuckers.*
- Mahogany neck, rosewood fingerboard; 24.75-inch scale, 22 frets; truss-rod adjuster at headstock; three-tuners-per-side black-face headstock; neck matches body colour.
- Solid single-cutaway body; black or red.
- Two black coverless humbuckers.
- Four controls (two volume, two tone) and three-way selector, all on body; side-mounted output jack.
- Black plastic pickguard.
- Six-saddle slim bridge, separate slim tailpiece.

Series 24.
034-5000
Indonesia

M-70 (13) 2002–05 *Three-tuners-per-side headstock, glued-in neck, dot markers, single-cutaway bound body, two black humbuckers.*
Similar to M-50 (see previous listing), except:
- Mahogany glued-in neck, bound rosewood fingerboard; diamond motif on black-face headstock.
- Solid single-cutaway bound body; black or blue.
- Two black coverless humbuckers.

Series 24.
034-7000
Korea

M-77 (13) 2002–05 *Three-tuners-per-side headstock, glued-in neck, block markers, single-cutaway bound body, two black humbuckers.*
Similar to M-50 (see earlier listing), except:
- Mahogany glued-in neck, bound rosewood fingerboard, block markers; diamond motif on black-face headstock.
- Solid single-cutaway bound body with figured front; sunburst, black, or red.
- Two black coverless humbuckers.
- Black laminate plastic pickguard.

Series 24.
034-7700
Korea

M-77 GOLD TOP LE (13) 2003–05 *Three-tuners-per-side headstock, glued-in neck, block markers, single-cutaway bound body with gold front.*

Similar to M-50 (see earlier listing), except:
- Mahogany glued-in neck, bound rosewood fingerboard, block markers; diamond motif on black-face headstock.
- Solid single-cutaway bound body; gold front only.
- Two metal-cover humbuckers.
- Cream plastic pickguard.

Series 24.
Limited Edition.
034-7700
Korea

M-80 (14) 2005–07 *"M-80" on three-tuners-per-side headstock, glued-in neck, slim block markers, two metal-cover humbuckers.*
- Mahogany glued-in neck, rosewood fingerboard, slim block markers; 24.75-inch scale, 22 frets; truss-rod adjuster at headstock; three-tuners-per-side black-face headstock; neck matches body colour.
- Solid short-horned offset-double-cutaway body; amber, black, or red.
- Two metal-cover humbuckers.
- Four controls (two volume, two tone) and three-way selector, all on body; side-mounted output jack.
- Six-saddle slim bridge, separate slim tailpiece.

Master Series.
034-4100
Korea

M-80 SPECIAL (14) 2005–07 *"M-80" on three-tuners-per-side headstock, bolt-on neck, no markers, two black humbuckers.*
Similar to M-80 (see previous listing), except:
- Mahogany bolt-on neck, no position markers.
- Body black, brown, or red.
- Two black coverless humbuckers.

Master Series.
034-4000
Indonesia

MINI (20) 1999–current *"Mini" on headstock.*
- Maple neck, rosewood fingerboard; 20.75-inch scale, 20 frets; truss-rod adjuster at headstock; two string-guides.
- Solid scaled-down slab offset-double-cutaway body; black, pink, or red.
- Three white six-polepiece pickups (bridge pickup angled).
- Two controls (volume, tone) and five-way selector, all on pickguard; output jack in body front.
- White plastic pickguard.
- Six-saddle small bridge/tailpiece.

031-0100 & 031-0101
China, Indonesia

MINI PLAYER (20) 2007–10 *"Mini" on headstock, speaker on body.*
- Maple neck, rosewood fingerboard; 20.75-inch scale, 20 frets; truss-rod adjuster at headstock; two string-guides.
- Solid scaled-down slab offset-double-cutaway body; black.
- One black coverless humbucker (at bridge).
- Two controls (volume, distortion) and speaker on body; side-

mounted output jack and headphone jack.
- Six-saddle small bridge/tailpiece.

030-0105

Indonesia

MUSICMASTER (6) 1998–99 *"Musicmaster" on headstock.*
- "Vista Series" on headstock.
- Maple neck, rosewood fingerboard; 24.75-inch scale, 22 frets; truss-rod adjuster at headstock; one string-guide; headstock face matches body colour.
- Solid slab offset-waist offset-double-cutaway body; various colours.
- One black coverless humbucker (at bridge).
- One control (volume) with push/pull-switch, and output jack, both on pickguard.
- White laminate plastic pickguard.
- Six-saddle small bridge with through-body stringing.

033-0100

China

S-65 (15) 2002–05 *Three-tuners-per-side headstock, bolt-on neck, bevelled-edge offset-double-cutaway body, two black humbuckers.*
- Mahogany neck, rosewood fingerboard; 24.75-inch scale, 22 frets; truss-rod adjuster at headstock; three-tuners-per-side black-face headstock; neck matches body colour.
- Solid bevelled-edge offset-double-cutaway body; black or red.
- Two black coverless humbuckers.
- Four controls (two volume, two tone), three-way selector, and output jack, all on body.
- Black plastic pickguard.
- Six-saddle slim bridge, separate slim tailpiece.

Series 24.

034-6500

Indonesia

S-73 (15) 2002–05 *Three-tuners-per-side headstock, glued-in neck, bevelled-edge offset-double-cutaway body, two black humbuckers.*
Similar to S-65 (see previous listing), except:
- Mahogany glued-in neck, bound rosewood fingerboard, block markers; diamond motif on black-face headstock.
- Two black coverless humbuckers.
- Black laminate plastic pickguard.

Series 24.

034-7300

Korea

SHOWMASTER H CAT GUITAR SLE (11) 2003–04
"Showmaster" on reverse headstock, cat's eyes and claw scratch graphics on body front, one black humbucker.
Similar to SHOWMASTER HH (see later listing), except:
- Two string-guides; no locking nut; claw scratch graphic on headstock face.
- Body black only with cat's eyes and claw scratch graphics on front.

- One black coverless humbucker (at bridge).
- One control (volume).
- Six-saddle small bridge with through-body stringing.

Special Limited Edition.

032-2800

China

SHOWMASTER H JIMMY SHAND SLE (21) 2003
"Showmaster" on perverse headstock, plaid pattern on body front, one black humbucker.
Similar to SHOWMASTER HH (see later listing), except:
- Two string-guides; no locking nut.
- Body black only with plaid pattern on front.
- One black coverless humbucker (at bridge).
- Two controls (volume, tone).
- Six-saddle small bridge with through-body stringing.

Scottish Limited Edition.

041-0104

Scotland

SHOWMASTER H JIMMY SHINE SLE (11) 2003–04
"Showmaster" on reverse headstock, Jimmy Shine graphic on body front, one black humbucker.
Similar to SHOWMASTER HH (see next listing), except:
- Two string-guides; no locking nut.
- Body black only with Jimmy Shine graphic on front.
- One black coverless humbucker (at bridge).
- Two controls (volume, tone).
- Six-saddle small bridge with through-body stringing.

Special Limited Edition.

032-2801

China

SHOWMASTER HH (11) 2002 *"Showmaster" on reverse headstock, 24 frets, two black humbuckers.*
- "Standard Series" on headstock.
- Maple neck, rosewood fingerboard; 24 frets; truss-rod adjuster at headstock; single-bar string-guide; locking nut; reverse headstock, face matches body colour.
- Solid slim-horned offset-double-cutaway body; black only.
- Two black coverless humbuckers.
- Two controls (volume, tone) and three-way selector, all on body; side-mounted output jack.
- Two-pivot locking bridge/vibrato unit.
- Black-plated metalwork.

132-3800

China

SHOWMASTER HH DELUXE (11) 2002 *"Showmaster" on reverse headstock, through-neck, 24 frets, two black humbuckers.*
Similar to SHOWMASTER HH (see previous listing), except:
- Maple through-neck, rosewood fingerboard; neck and headstock face match body colour.
- Body red only.

132-4800

China.

SHOWMASTER HH GHOST FLAMES SLE (11) 2002–03
"Showmaster" on reverse headstock, flames graphic on body front.
Similar to SHOWMASTER HH (see earlier listing), except:
- Body various colours with black or white flames graphic on front.
Special Limited Edition.
132-3200
China

SHOWMASTER HH GRAFITTI YELLOW SLE (11) 2003
"Showmaster" on reverse headstock, yellow finish.
Similar to SHOWMASTER HH (see earlier listing), except:
- Body yellow only.
Special Limited Edition.
132-3100
China

SHOWMASTER HH HOLOFLAKE SLE (11) 2003
"Showmaster" on reverse headstock, holoflake finish, six-saddle bridge with through-body stringing.
Similar to SHOWMASTER HH (see earlier listing), except:
- Two string-guides; no locking nut.
- Body 'Holoflake' (reflective speckled blue/green/pink etc) only.
- Six-saddle small bridge with through-body stringing.
Special Limited Edition.
032-2600
China

SHOWMASTER HH RALLY STRIPE (11) 2003–05
"Showmaster" on three-tuners-per-side headstock, striped body.
- Maple neck, rosewood fingerboard; 24 frets; truss-rod adjuster at headstock; three-tuners-per-side black-face headstock.
- Solid slim-horned offset-double-cutaway body; black with red stripes or silver with black stripes.
- Two black coverless humbuckers.
- Two controls (two volume) and three-way selector, all on body; side-mounted output jack.
- Six-saddle small bridge with through-body stringing.
- Black-plated metalwork.
032-3600
China

SHOWMASTER HH SKULL & CROSSBONES (11) 2003–05
"Showmaster" on reverse headstock, skull & crossbones graphic on body front.
Similar to SHOWMASTER HH (see earlier listing), except:
- Rosewood fingerboard, skull & crossbones position markers.
- Body black only with skull & crossbones graphic on front.
132-3300
China

SHOWMASTER HS BLACKOUT (11) 2003–04 *"Showmaster" on reverse headstock, one black humbucker and one black single-coil, two-pivot bridge/vibrato unit.*

- Maple neck, rosewood fingerboard; 24 frets; truss-rod adjuster at headstock; two string-guides; reverse headstock with black face.
- Solid slim-horned offset-double-cutaway body; black only.
- One black coverless humbucker (at bridge) and one black six-polepiece pickup (at neck).
- Two controls (volume, tone) and three-way selector, all on body; side-mounted output jack.
- Two-pivot bridge/vibrato unit.
- Black-plated metalwork.
Also known as BLACKOUT SHOWMASTER HS.
032-3300
China

SHOWMASTER HS JASON ELLIS SIGNATURE (11)
2002–05 *"Showmaster" on reverse headstock, 'balance' graphic on body front, one black humbucker and one black single-coil.*
Similar to SHOWMASTER HH (see earlier listing), except:
- Body black or red with Jason Ellis 'balance' graphic on front.
- One black coverless humbucker (at bridge) and one black six-polepiece pickup (at neck).
132-3000
China

SHOWMASTER HSH (11) 2002–03 *"Showmaster" on reverse headstock, 24 frets, two black humbuckers and one black single-coil.*
Similar to SHOWMASTER HH (see earlier listing), except:
- Body blue only.
- Two black coverless humbuckers and one black six-polepiece pickup (in centre).
- Two controls (volume, tone) and five-way selector.
132-3900
China

SHOWMASTER HSH DELUXE (11) 2002 *"Showmaster" on reverse headstock, through-neck, 24 frets, two black humbuckers and one black single-coil.*
Similar to SHOWMASTER HSH (see previous listing), except:
- Maple through-neck, rosewood fingerboard; neck and headstock face match body colour.
- Body black only.
132-4900
China.

SHOWMASTER HSS (11) 2002–03 *"Showmaster" on reverse headstock, 24 frets, one black humbucker and two black single-coils.*
Similar to SHOWMASTER HH (see earlier listing), except:
- Body black or blue.
- One black coverless humbucker (at bridge) and two black six-polepiece pickups.
- Two controls (volume, tone) and five-way selector.
132-3700 & 132-3500
China, Indonesia

SHOWMASTER HSS NLT (11) 2002–04 *"Showmaster" on reverse headstock, 22 frets, one black humbucker and two black single-coils.*
- Maple neck, rosewood fingerboard; 22 frets; truss-rod adjuster at headstock; two string-guides; reverse headstock.
- Solid slim-horned offset-double-cutaway body; black or blue.
- One black coverless humbucker (at bridge) and two black six-polepiece pickups.
- Two controls (volume, tone) and five-way selector, all on body; side-mounted output jack.
- Two-pivot bridge/vibrato unit.
032-2700
China, Indonesia

SHOWMASTER HSS NLT JACK DANIELS (11) 2004
"Showmaster" on reverse headstock, Jack Daniels graphics on black body.
Similar to SHOWMASTER HSS NLT (see previous listing), except:
- Body black only with Jack Daniels graphics on front.
Part Number not known
Indonesia.

STAGEMASTER HH first version (11) 1999–2000
"Stagemaster" on reverse headstock, 22 frets, two white humbuckers.
- "Standard Series" on headstock.
- Maple neck, rosewood fingerboard; 22 frets; truss-rod adjuster at headstock; single-bar string-guide; locking nut; reverse headstock.
- Solid slim-horned offset-double-cutaway body; various colours.
- Two white coverless humbuckers.
- Two controls (volume, tone) and three-way selector, all on pickguard; output jack in body face.
- White laminate plastic pickguard.
- Two-pivot locking bridge/vibrato unit.
132-2800
China

STAGEMASTER HH second version (11) 2000–02
"Stagemaster" on reverse headstock, 24 frets, two black humbuckers.
- "Standard Series" on headstock.
- Maple neck, rosewood fingerboard; 24 frets; truss-rod adjuster at headstock; single-bar string-guide; locking nut; reverse headstock, face matches body colour.
- Solid slim-horned offset-double-cutaway body; black, blue, or purple.
- Two black coverless humbuckers.
- Two controls (volume, tone) and three-way selector, all on body; side-mounted output jack.
- Two-pivot locking bridge/vibrato unit.
- Black-plated metalwork.
132-3800
China

STAGEMASTER HH DELUXE (11) 2000–02 *"Stagemaster" on reverse headstock, through-neck, 24 frets, two black humbuckers.*
Similar to STAGEMASTER HH second version (see previous listing), except:
- Maple through-neck, rosewood fingerboard; neck and headstock face match body colour.
- Body blue, gold, or red.
132-4800
China.

STAGEMASTER HH 7 FR seven-string (11) 2000–02
"Stagemaster" on reverse seven-string headstock, 24 frets, two black humbuckers, locking bridge/vibrato system.
- "Standard Series" on headstock.
- Maple neck, rosewood fingerboard; 24 frets; truss-rod adjuster at headstock; single-bar string-guide; locking nut; seven-string reverse headstock, face matches body colour.
- Solid slim-horned offset-double-cutaway body; black, blue, or purple.
- Two black coverless humbuckers.
- Two controls (volume, tone) and three-way selector, all on body; side-mounted output jack.
- Two-pivot locking bridge/vibrato unit.
- Black-plated metalwork.
132-3807
China

STAGEMASTER HH 7 HT seven-string (11) 2000–02
"Stagemaster" on reverse seven-string headstock, 24 frets, two black humbuckers, seven-saddle bridge with through-body stringing.
Similar to STAGEMASTER 7 FR (see previous listing), except:
- Two string-guides; no locking nut.
- Seven-saddle small bridge with through-body stringing.
032-3837
China

STAGEMASTER HSH first version (11) 1999–2000
"Stagemaster" on reverse headstock, 22 frets, two white humbuckers and one white single-coil.
Similar to STAGEMASTER HH first version (see earlier listing), except:
- Two white coverless humbuckers and one white six-polepiece pickup (in centre).
- Two controls (volume, tone) and five-way selector.
132-2900
China

STAGEMASTER HSH second version (11) 2000–02
"Stagemaster" on reverse headstock, 24 frets, two black humbuckers and one black single-coil.
Similar to STAGEMASTER HH second version (see earlier listing), except:
- Two black coverless humbuckers and one black six-polepiece pickup (in centre).

■ Two controls (volume, tone) and five-way selector.
132-3900
China

STAGEMASTER HSH DELUXE (11) 2000–02 *"Stagemaster" on reverse headstock, 24 frets, through-neck, two black humbuckers and one black single-coil.*
Similar to STAGEMASTER HSH second version (see previous listing), except:
■ Maple through-neck, rosewood fingerboard; neck and headstock face match body colour.
■ Body black, grey, or green.
■ Two black coverless humbuckers and one black six-polepiece pickup (in centre).
■ Two controls (volume, tone) and five-way selector.
132-4900
China.

STAGEMASTER HSS first version (11) 1999–2000
"Stagemaster" on reverse headstock, 22 frets, one black humbucker and two white single-coils.
Similar to STAGEMASTER HH first version (see earlier listing), except:
■ One white coverless humbucker (at bridge) and two white six-polepiece pickups.
■ Two controls (volume, tone) and five-way selector.
132-2700
China

STAGEMASTER HSS second version (11) 2000–02
"Stagemaster" on reverse headstock, 24 frets, one black humbucker and two black single-coils.
Similar to STAGEMASTER HH second version (see earlier listing), except:
■ One black coverless humbucker (at bridge) and two black six-polepiece pickups.
■ Two controls (volume, tone) and five-way selector.
132-3700
China

STAGEMASTER HSS NLT (11) 2001–02 *"Stagemaster" on reverse headstock, 22 frets, one black humbucker and two black single-coils.*
■ Maple neck, rosewood fingerboard; 22 frets; truss-rod adjuster at headstock; two string-guides; reverse headstock.
■ Solid slim-horned offset-double-cutaway body; black, blue, or purple.
■ One black coverless humbucker (at bridge) and two black six-polepiece pickups.
■ Two controls (volume, tone) and five-way selector, all on body; side-mounted output jack.
■ Two-pivot bridge/vibrato unit.
032-2700
China

STARFIRE (16) 2002–05 *Three-tuners-per-side headstock,*

glued-in neck, semi-acoustic twin-cutaway body, two humbuckers.
■ Mahogany glued-in neck, bound rosewood fingerboard; 24.75-inch scale, 22 frets; truss-rod adjuster at headstock; three-tuners-per-side black-face headstock with diamond motif; neck matches body colour.
■ Semi-acoustic twin-cutaway bound body with two f-holes; natural or red.
■ Two metal-cover or black coverless humbuckers.
■ Four controls (two volume, two tone), three-way selector, and output jack, all on body.
■ Black laminate plastic pickguard.
■ Six-saddle slim bridge, separate slim tailpiece.
Series 24.
034-2000
Korea

SUB-SONIC baritone (11) 2001–02 *"Sub-Sonic" on reverse headstock, 24 frets, through-neck, two black humbuckers.*
■ "Standard Series" on headstock.
■ Maple through-neck, rosewood fingerboard; 27-inch scale, 24 frets; truss-rod adjuster at headstock; two string-guides; reverse headstock; neck and headstock face match body colour.
■ Solid slim-horned offset-double-cutaway body; black only.
■ Two black coverless humbuckers.
■ Two controls (volume, tone) and three-way selector, all on body; side-mounted output jack.
■ Six-saddle small bridge with through-body stringing.
■ Black-plated metalwork.
032-4805
China

SUPER-SONIC (17) 1997–98 *"Super-Sonic" on reverse headstock.*
■ "Vista Series" on headstock.
■ Maple neck, rosewood fingerboard; 24-inch scale, 22 frets; 'bullet' truss-rod adjuster at headstock; two string-guides; reverse enlarged (70s-style) headstock.
■ Solid smaller contoured offset-waist reverse body; various colours.
■ Two black coverless humbuckers (bridge pickup angled).
■ Two controls (both volume) and output jack on metal plate adjoining pickguard; three-way selector on pickguard.
■ White laminate plastic pickguard.
■ Six-pivot bridge/vibrato unit.
027-1500
Japan

VENUS (18) 1997–98 *"Venus" on headstock.*
■ "Vista Series" on headstock.
■ Maple neck, bound rosewood fingerboard; 22 frets; truss-rod adjuster at headstock; one string-guide; headstock face matches body colour.
■ Solid contoured offset-waist double-cutaway body; black or green.

- One white coverless humbucker (angled at bridge) and one white six-polepiece pickup (angled at neck).
- One control (volume), three-way selector, and output jack, all on pickguard.
- White pearl laminate plastic pickguard.
- Six-saddle slim bridge, separate through-body stringing.

027-1700
Japan

VENUS XII 12-string (18) 1997–98 *"Venus" on 12-string headstock.* Similar to VENUS (see previous listing), except:
- One 'bracket' string-guide; six-tuners-per-side headstock, face matches body colour.
- Two white plain-top split pickups.
- Two controls (volume, tone), three-way selector, and output jack, all on pickguard.
- 12-saddle bridge with through-body stringing.

027-1800
Japan

VINTAGE MODIFIED JAGUAR HH (10) 2011–current *"Jaguar" on headstock, two black/white humbuckers.*
- Maple neck, rosewood fingerboard; 24-inch scale, 22 frets; truss-rod adjuster at headstock; one string-guide.
- Solid contoured offset-waist body; sunburst or red.
- Two black/white coverless humbuckers.
- Two dual-concentric controls (each volume, tone) and three-way selector, all on pickguard; output jack in body front.
- Brown shell laminate plastic pickguard.
- Six-saddle small bridge/tailpiece with angled sides.

030-2700
Indonesia

VINTAGE MODIFIED JAZZMASTER (10) 2011–current *"Jazzmaster" on headstock, maple fingerboard.*
- Maple neck, maple fingerboard; truss-rod adjuster at headstock; one string-guide.
- Solid contoured offset-waist body; sunburst or butterscotch.
- Two large white or black six-polepiece pickups.
- Two dual-concentric controls (each volume, tone) and three-way selector, all on pickguard; output jack in body front.
- White laminate or black plastic pickguard.
- Six-saddle small bridge/tailpiece with angled sides.

030-2800
Indonesia

X-155 (19) 2002–05 *Three-tuners-per-side headstock, glued-in neck, hollow single-cutaway body, two humbuckers.*
- Mahogany glued-in neck, bound rosewood fingerboard, block markers; 24.75-inch scale, 22 frets; truss-rod adjuster at headstock; three-tuners-per-side black-face headstock with diamond motif; neck matches body colour.
- Hollow single-cutaway bound body with two f-holes; sunburst or natural.
- Two metal-cover or black coverless humbuckers.
- Four controls (two volume, two tone) and three-way selector on body; side-mounted output jack.
- Black laminate plastic pickguard.
- Single-saddle wooden bridge, separate trapeze tailpiece with "S" logo.

Series 24.
034-1500
Korea

X-155 WHITE HEAT SE (19) 2003–05 *Three-tuners-per-side headstock, glued-in neck, hollow single-cutaway body with white flame pattern on front.*
Similar to X-155 (see previous listing), except:
- Body black or blue, both with white flame graphic on front.
- Black laminate pickguard or no pickguard.

Special Edition.
Series 24.
034-1500
Korea

'51 (1) 2004–07 *Telecaster-style headstock, one black humbucker and one angled single-coil, two controls on small metal plate.*
- Maple neck, maple fingerboard; truss-rod adjuster at headstock; two string-guides; Telecaster-style headstock.
- Solid contoured offset-double-cutaway body; sunburst, black, or blonde.
- One black coverless humbucker (at bridge) and one black or white six-polepiece pickup (angled at neck).
- One control (volume) with push/pull-switch and three-way rotary selector, both on metal plate adjoining pickguard; side-mounted output jack.
- Black or white plastic pickguard.
- Six-saddle small bridge/tailpiece.

Also body in red or blue (sold in Japan only).
032-5100
Indonesia

SQUIER-RELATED BRANDS

Rogue By Squier

This brandname appeared on instruments produced by Fender for a US retailer. Built in China and Indonesia, they debuted during 1999. The limited line comprised two Stratocaster-based six-strings, the ST-3 and ST-4. The ST-3 featured three single-coil pickups; the ST-4 substituted a humbucker for the bridge-position single-coil.

Squier II

This brandname was introduced in 1988, when Fender decided to target an even lower price level of the electric guitar market. Production was sourced mainly from various factories in Korea, although some early Squier II examples originated in India. The range comprised models based on established designs, essentially more economy-conscious equivalents of existing

Squier six-strings. The Standard Stratocaster was initially offered in two versions, with either three single-coils or a humbucker plus two single-coils. The latter later became the Contemporary model, to eliminate any confusion. The Squier II catalogue was completed by a standard-specification Telecaster. The line lasted until 1992, when it was superseded by equally affordable Squier-brand instruments.

DATING SQUIER GUITARS

Putting a date to an instrument is important, not only because it helps to satisfy our natural curiosity regarding age, but in the case of more desirable guitars, the year of production can affect value. However, the span of Squier production is significantly shorter than that of Fender, so 'vintage' considerations are less relevant. In addition, Squier is a less expensive brand and, therefore, most models do not command the same levels of prices and interest accorded to Fender guitars.

There are very few easily recognisable changes to construction or components that have any chronological significance across all Squier models. Instead, you need to use other information to determine the age of an instrument, and these are shown in this section.

SERIES NAME

Although not always present, the name of a series appears on the headstock of certain Squier instruments, in addition to the brand logo and model name. When present, a series name can indicate the period of production, although it will not pinpoint a specific year. In addition, some series are specific to certain countries and therefore help to identify the manufacturing source.

Name	Country of origin	Production span
Affinity Series	Various	1997–current
Bullet Series	Korea	1994–95
Bullet Series	China	1995–97
California Series	China	2003–current
Pro Tone Series	Korea	1996–98
Silver Series	Japan	1992–94
Squier Series	Japan	1982
Squier Series	Korea	1992–94
Squier Series	Mexico	1994–96
Standard Series	Various	1999–current
Vista Series	Japan	1997–98

SERIAL NUMBERS

With Squier, serial numbers are particularly important because for many instruments there are few other dating clues. Apart from providing an indication of production period, a serial number can confirm the country of origin, which is usually shown somewhere on the guitar. There are details of how to check the country of origin on page 126. Once you've done that, look under the country below to decode the serial number. Depending on the instrument's age and origin, the serial number will be on the headstock face or back, on the neck heel (the rear flat section near the body joint), or on the neck-plate (the metal plate on the back of the body at the neck joint). We've combined our comprehensive research with information supplied by Fender to provide as accurate a guide as possible.

There are details of how to check the country of origin on page 126.

CHINA (1995–current)

Instruments usually carry the description "Made In China" or "Crafted In China".

CA prefix ("Made In China" or "Crafted In China")
The first figure of the following number provides the production period, but manufacture may continue into the next year or years.

CAE– prefix (no country shown)
The first two figures of a following ten-digit number provide the production period, but manufacture may continue into the next year or years.
For example: **CAE–**0020901374 = 2000–01

CD prefix ("Made In China" or "Crafted In China")
The first figure of the following number provides the production period, but manufacture may continue into the next year or years.

CGRL prefix ("Crafted In China")
The first two figures of a following eight-digit number provide the production period, but manufacture may continue into the next year or years.
For example: **CGRL**0811718 = 2008–09

CGS prefix ("Crafted In China")
The first two figures of a following seven or eight or nine-digit number provide the production period, but manufacture may continue into the next year or years.
For example: **CGS**1037233 = 2010–11
CGS11008091 = 2011–12
CGS080100764 = 2008–09

CJ prefix ("Made In China" or "Crafted In China")
The first figure of the following number provides the production period, but manufacture may continue into the next year or years.

CO prefix ("Crafted In China")
The first figure of a following eight-digit number provides the production period, but manufacture may continue into the next year or years.
For example: **CO**8074283 = 1998–99

COB prefix ("Crafted In China")
The first two figures of a following nine-digit number provide the production period, but manufacture may continue into the next year or years.
For example: **COB**081176008 = 2008–09

COS prefix ("Crafted In China")
The first two figures of a following eight-digit number provide the production period, but manufacture may continue into the next year or years.
For example: **COS**10020472 = 2010–11

CT prefix ("Made In China" or "Crafted In China")
The first figure of the following number provides the production period, but manufacture may continue into the next year or years.

CXS prefix ("Crafted In China")
The first two figures of a following nine-digit number provide the production period, but manufacture may continue into the next year or years.
For example: **CXS**071055118 = 2007–08

CY prefix ("Crafted In China")
The first figure of a following eight-digit number provides the production period, but manufacture may continue into the next year or years.
For example: **CY**20712281 = 2002–03
CY41117413 = 2004–05
CY81011071 = 2008–09

CY prefix ("Crafted In China")
The first two figures of a following eight or nine-digit number provide the production period, but manufacture may continue into the next year or years.
For example: **CY**98076960 = 1998–99
CY080100764 = 2008–09

NC prefix ("Made In China")
The first figure of a following six-digit number provides the production period, but manufacture may continue into the next year or years.
For example: **NC**730607 = 1997–98

YN prefix ("Made In China")
The first figure of a following six-digit number provides the production period, but manufacture may continue into the next year or years.
For example: **YN**714187 = 1997–98

INDIA (2007–current)

Instruments usually carry the description "Crafted In India".

Prefix	Number	Production period
CS	07 + 6 digits	2007–08
NHS	10 + 5 digits	2010–11
NHS	11 + 5 digits	2011–12
NSHA	09 + 6 digits	2009–10
NSHD	09 + 6 digits	2009–10
NSHE	09 + 6 digits	2009–10
NSHF	09 + 6 digits	2009–10
NHSG	09 + 6 digits	2009–10
NSHH	09 + 6 digits	2009–10
NSHI	09 + 6 digits	2009–10
NSHJ	08 + 6 digits	2008–09
NSHJ	09 + 6 digits	2009–10
NSHK	09 + 6 digits	2009–10
SH	07 + 6 digits	2007–08
SH	08 + 6 digits	2008–09
ZSSH	07 + 6 digits	2007–08
ZSSH	08 + 6 digits	2008–09

INDONESIA (1996–current)

Instruments usually carry the description "Crafted In Indonesia".

IC prefix ("Crafted In Indonesia")
The first two figures of a following eight or nine-digit number provide the production period, but manufacture may continue into the next year or years.
For example: **IC**98123832 = 1998–99
IC050844159 = 2005–06
ICS10187570 = 2010–11

ICS prefix ("Crafted In Indonesia")
The first two figures of a following eight or nine-digit number provide the production period, but manufacture may continue into the next year or years.

IS prefix ("Crafted In Indonesia")
The first two figures of a following eight or nine-digit number provide the production period, but manufacture may continue into the next year or years.
For example: **IS**00094016 = 2000–01

SI prefix ("Crafted In Indonesia")
The first two figures of a following eight or nine-digit number provide the production period, but manufacture may continue into the next year or years.
For example: **SI**02080634 = 2002–03
SI050701136 = 2005–06

JAPAN (1982–98)

Instruments usually carry the description "Made In Japan" or "Crafted In Japan".

The serial number system is the same as that used on Japanese-made Fender instruments, with each prefix denoting a different production period. Japanese-made Squier models were officially exported from 1982–88, 1992–94, and 1996–98, but manufacture for the Japanese domestic market was continuous. It should be noted that all dates are approximate and that there are significant duplications, overlaps, and disparities.

"Made In Japan" (1982–97)

Prefix	Number	Production period
A	6 digits	1985–86
B	6 digits	1985–86
C	6 digits	1985–86
E	6 digits	1984–87
F	6 digits	1986–87
G	6 digits	1987–88
H	6 digits	1988–89
I	6 digits	1989–90
J	6 digits	1989–90
JV	5 digits	1982–84
K	6 digits	1990–91
L	6 digits	1991–92
M	6 digits	1992–93
N	6 digits	1993–94
P	6 digits	1993–94
Q	6 digits	1993–94
S	6 digits	1994–95
SQ	5 digits	1983–84
T	6 digits	1994–95
U	6 digits	1995–96
V	6 digits	1996–97

"Crafted In Japan" (1995–2008)

Prefix	Number	Production period
A	6 digits	1997–98
B	6 digits	1998–99
N	5 digits	1995–96
O	6 digits	1997–2000
P	6 digits	1999–2002
Q	6 digits	2002–04
R	6 digits	2004–06
S	6 digits	2006–08
T	6 digits	2007–08

"Made In Japan" (2007–current)

Prefix	Number	Production period
T	6 digits	2007–10
U	6 digits	2010–current

KOREA (1988–98)

Instruments usually carry the description "Made In Korea" or "Crafted In Korea".

CN prefix ("Made In Korea" or "Crafted In Korea")
"N" indicates the Nineties (1990s). The first figure of a following six-digit number provides the production period, but manufacture may continue into the next year or years.
For example: **CN**451743 = 1994–95

E prefix ("Made In Korea")
The first figure of a following six or seven-digit number provides the production period, but manufacture may continue into the next year or years.
For example: **E**724049 = 1987–88
　　　　　　 E974185 = 1989–90
　　　　　　 E1012982 = 1991–92

KC prefix ("Made In Korea" or "Crafted In Korea")
The first two figures of a following eight-digit number provide the production period, but manufacture may continue into the next year or years.
For example: **KC**97070869 = 1997–98
　　　　　　 KC05057996 = 2005–06

KV prefix ("Made In Korea" or "Crafted In Korea")
The first two figures of a following eight-digit number provide the production period, but manufacture may continue into the next year or years.
For example: **KV**97081970 = 1997–98

M prefix ("Made In Korea")
The first figure of a following seven-digit number provides the production period, but manufacture may continue into the next year or years.
For example: **M**2730208 = 1992–93

NK prefix ("Made In Korea")
"N" indicates the Nineties (1990s).
The first figure of a following six-digit number provides the production period, but manufacture may continue into the next year or years.
For example: **NK**412055 = 1994

S prefix ("Made In Korea")
The first figure of a following six or seven-digit number provides the production period, but manufacture may continue into the next year or years.
For example: **S**976453 = 1989–90
　　　　　　 S1006470 = 1991–92

VN prefix ("Made In Korea")
"N" indicates the Nineties (1990s).
The first figure of a following six or seven-digit number provides the production period, but manufacture may continue into the next year or years.

For example: **VN**620364 = 1996–97
 VN2754709 = 1992–93

No prefix ("Crafted In Korea")
The first figure of a six or seven-digit serial number without a prefix provides the production period, but manufacture may continue into the next year or years.
For example: 713961 = 1997–98
 6115185 = 1996–97

MEXICO (1993–99)
Instruments usually carry the description "Made In Mexico".
The serial number system is the same as that used on Mexican-made Fender-brand instruments from this production period.

MN prefix ("Made In Mexico")
"M" confirms Mexican manufacture and "N" indicates the Nineties (1990s).
The first figure of a following six or seven-digit number provides

the production period, but manufacture may continue into the next year or years.
For example: **MN**576965 = 1995–96
 MN8106867 = 1998–99

USA (1991–93)
Instruments usually carry the description "Made In USA".
The serial number system is the same as that used on USA-made Fender-brand instruments from this production period.

E or N prefix ("Made In USA")
The first figure of a following six or seven-digit number provides the production period.
For example: **E**903132 = 1990–91

No prefix ("Made In USA")
A six-digit serial number starting with "0" (zero), rather than a letter prefix, also indicates 1991–93, but the number is located on the neck-plate, not the headstock.

PRODUCTION SOURCE CODES

In the 70s, Fender introduced a part number system, intended to make ordering and stock-keeping easier for the company and for its distributors and dealers. The ten-digit numbers are allocated to every Fender product, from individual components to complete instruments. They don't actually appear on the guitars themselves but are used throughout Fender catalogues and pricelists.

The part numbers can prove useful because they denote production details, including manufacturing source, model type, fingerboard wood, hardware options, and finish colour.

The same system applies to Squier instruments, with each version and variation of a guitar allotted a specific part number. The first digit is usually a "0", although this is a "1" for guitars fitted with a locking-type bridge/vibrato system. The next two digits indicate the country of origin, and we define this pairing as the production source code.

On the right are the production source codes allocated to Squier and Squier II instruments since the Squier brand began in 1982. You'll notice that in some cases the same two digits have denoted different countries at different times.

Squier

Code	Source
13	Mexico
14	USA
25	Japan
26	China, Japan
27	Japan, Korea
28	China
29	India
30	China, India, Indonesia
31	China, Indonesia
32	China, India, Indonesia, Japan, Korea
33	China, Indonesia, Japan, Korea
34	China, Indonesia, Korea

Squier II

Code	Source
28	India
29	Korea
33	India

MODEL CHRONOLOGY

This list shows in chronological order of start date the Squier electric guitar models made from 1982 to 2011.

1982
FENDER SQUIER SERIES STRATOCASTER '57 1982
FENDER SQUIER SERIES STRATOCASTER '62 1982
FENDER SQUIER SERIES TELECASTER '52 1982

1983
BULLET H-2 1983–86
BULLET S-3 1983–86

BULLET S-3T first version 1983–85
STRATOCASTER (aka POPULAR) 1983–84
TELECASTER (aka POPULAR) 1983–84

1985
CONTEMPORARY BULLET HST first version 1985–86
CONTEMPORARY STRATOCASTER H 1985–88
CONTEMPORARY STRATOCASTER HH 1985–87
KATANA 1985–87
STANDARD STRATOCASTER 1985–99
STANDARD TELECASTER 1985–99

1986

BULLET S-3T second version 1986–87
CONTEMPORARY BULLET HST second version 1986–87
CONTEMPORARY STRATOCASTER HSS 1986–88

1987

BULLET S-3T third version 1987–88
CONTEMPORARY BULLET HST third version 1987–88
STANDARD STRATOCASTER string-clamp 1987–88

1988

BULLET SERIES STRATOCASTER 1988–97
CONTEMPORARY STRATOCASTER first version 1988–91

1989

H.M. I 1989–93
H.M. II 1989–93
H.M. III 1989–93

1990

H.M. IV 1990–93
H.M. V 1990–93

1992

CONTEMPORARY STRATOCASTER second version 1992–94
FENDER SQUIER SERIES STRATOCASTER 1992–96
FENDER SQUIER SERIES TELECASTER 1992–96
FLOYD ROSE STANDARD STRATOCASTER first version 1992–96
FR-211 1992–94
FR-211ST 1992–94
FR-212 1992–94
HANK MARVIN STRATOCASTER 1992–93
H.M. TELE 1992–93
SILVER SERIES STRATOCASTER 1992–94
SILVER SERIES TELECASTER 1992–94
SPECIAL STRATOCASTER 1992–93
WAYNE'S WORLD STRATOCASTER first version 1992–93

1993

CLASSIC STRATOCASTER 1993–94
WAYNE'S WORLD STRATOCASTER second version 1993
WAYNE'S WORLD STRATOCASTER FLOYD ROSE 1993

1994

FLOYD ROSE STANDARD STRATOCASTER second version 1994–96

1995

BULLET first version 1995–96

1996

PRO TONE FAT STRAT 1996–98
PRO TONE FAT TELE 1996–98
PRO TONE STRATOCASTER 1996–98
PRO TONE THINLINE TELE 1996–98
STANDARD FAT STRAT first version 1996–98
TRADITION/TRADITIONAL STRATOCASTER 1996

TRADITION/TRADITIONAL TELECASTER 1996

1997

AFFINITY STRATOCASTER 1997–current
AFFINITY TELECASTER 1997–current
JAGMASTER first version 1997–98
SUPER-SONIC 1997–98
VENUS 1997–98
VENUS XII 12-string 1997–98

1998

DUO-SONIC 1998–99
MUSICMASTER 1998–99
STANDARD FAT STRAT second version 1998–99
STANDARD FAT STRAT FLOYD ROSE 1998–99

1999

MINI 1999–current
STAGEMASTER HH first version 1999–2000
STAGEMASTER HSH first version 1999–2000
STAGEMASTER HSS first version 1999–2000
STANDARD DOUBLE FAT STRAT first version 1999–2000
STANDARD FAT STRAT third version 1999–2000
STANDARD STRATOCASTER 1999–current
STANDARD TELECASTER 1999–current

2000

BULLET second version 2000–07
JAGMASTER second version 2000–04
STAGEMASTER HH second version 2000–02
STAGEMASTER HH DELUXE 2000–02
STAGEMASTER HH 7 FR seven-string 2000–02
STAGEMASTER HH 7 HT seven-string 2000–02
STAGEMASTER HSH second version 2000–02
STAGEMASTER HSS second version 2000–02
STAGEMASTER HSH DELUXE 2000–02
STANDARD DOUBLE FAT STRAT second version 2000–07
STANDARD DOUBLE FAT STRAT 7 HT 2000–02
STANDARD FAT STRAT fourth version 2000–06
STANDARD FAT STRAT 7 2000–02
STANDARD FAT TELECASTER 2000–07

2001

STRAT HSS 2001–current
DOUBLE FAT TELECASTER DELUXE 2001–03
FAT STRAT FSR first version 2001–07
FAT STRAT MAPLE FSR 2001–07
STAGEMASTER HSS NLT 2001–02
STRAT HSS 2001–current
SUB-SONIC baritone 2001–02

2002

BULLET SPECIAL 2002–07
SHOWMASTER HS JASON ELLIS SIGNATURE 2002–05
M-50 2002–05 / M-70 2002–05 / M-77 2002–05
S-65 2002–05 / S-73 2002–05

SHOWMASTER HH 2002
SHOWMASTER HH DELUXE 2002
SHOWMASTER HH GHOST FLAMES SLE 2002–03
SHOWMASTER HSH 2002–03
SHOWMASTER HSH DELUXE 2002
SHOWMASTER HSS 2002–03
SHOWMASTER HSS NLT 2002–04
STARFIRE 2002–05
TOM DELONGE STRATOCASTER 2002–03
X-155 2002–05

2003
BULLET DELUXE 2003–04
CALIFORNIA FAT STRAT first version 2003–current
CALIFORNIA FAT STRAT second version 2003–current
CALIFORNIA STRATOCASTER 2003–current
CALIFORNIA TELECASTER 2003–current
CYCLONE 2003–07
M-77 GOLD TOP LE 2003–05
SHOWMASTER H CAT GUITAR SLE 2003–04
SHOWMASTER HH GRAFITTI YELLOW SLE 2003
SHOWMASTER HH HOLOFLAKE SLE 2003
SHOWMASTER HH RALLY STRIPE 2003–05
SHOWMASTER HH SKULL & CROSSBONES 2003–05
SHOWMASTER HS BLACKOUT 2003–04
SHOWMASTER H JIMMY SHINE SLE 2003–04
VINTAGE MODIFIED TELECASTER CUSTOM 2003–current
X-155 WHITE HEAT 2003–05

2004
BLACK & CHROME STANDARD STRATOCASTER 2004–current
BLACK & CHROME TELECASTER 2004–current
DELUXE FLAME TOP STRATOCASTER 2004–08
DELUXE QUILT TOP STRATOCASTER 2004–08
DELUXE STRATOCASTER 2004–current
HEINEKEN STRATOCASTER 2004–08
JACK DANIELS STRAT 2004–08
JACK DANIELS STRAT HSS 2004–08
MILLER GENUINE DRAFT STRATOCASTER 2004–08
MILLER LITE STRATOCASTER 2004–08
ROLLING ROCK STRATOCASTER 2004
SHOWMASTER HSS NLT JACK DANIELS 2004
TELE SPECIAL 2004–07
VINTAGE MODIFIED TELECASTER CUSTOM II 2004–current
'51 2004–07

2005
BLACK & CHROME FAT STRAT 2005–current
BULLET third version 2005–06
CHAMBERED TELE HH 2005–07
ESPRIT 2005–07
ICEHOUSE STRATOCASTER 2005
JAGMASTER third version 2005–current
M-80 2005–07
M-80 SPECIAL 2005–07
SATIN TRANS FAT STRATOCASTER HH 2005–07

SATIN TRANS FAT STRATOCASTER HSS 2005–07
SATIN TRANS STRATOCASTER 2005–07
THINLINE TELE HH 2005–07

2006
FAT STRAT FSR second version 2006–07
HELLO KITTY MINI 2006–09
HELLO KITTY STRAT 2006–09
OBEY GRAPHIC STRATOCASTER COLLAGE 2006–10
OBEY GRAPHIC STRATOCASTER DISSENT 2006–10
OBEY GRAPHIC TELECASTER COLLAGE 2006–10
OBEY GRAPHIC TELECASTER PROPAGANDA 2006–10
O-LARN SIGNATURE STRATOCASTER 2006–current

2007
AVRIL LAVIGNE TELECASTER 2007–current
BULLET STRAT WITH TREMOLO 2007–current
DELUXE HOT RAILS STRAT 2007–current
DERYCK WHIBLEY TELECASTER 2007–current
DETONATOR STRAT FSR 2007
MINI PLAYER 2007–10
STANDARD STRATOCASTER HSS 2007–current
VINTAGE MODIFIED STRAT HSS 2007–current
VINTAGE MODIFIED STRATOCASTER 2007–current
VINTAGE MODIFIED TELE SH 2007–current
VINTAGE MODIFIED TELE SSH 2007–current
VINTAGE MODIFIED TELECASTER THINLINE 2007–current

2008
CLASSIC VIBE DUO-SONIC 50s 2008–current
CLASSIC VIBE STRATOCASTER 2008–current
CLASSIC VIBE TELECASTER 2008–current
ROLLING ROCK TELECASTER 2008

2009
J5 TELECASTER 2009–current
SHAM KAMIKAZE STRATOCASTER 2009–current
SIMON NEIL STRATOCASTER 2009–current
STANDARD TELECASTER HS FSR 2009

2010
BULLET HH HT FSR 2010
BULLET HH WITH TREMOLO FSR 2010–11
BULLET STRAT HSS WITH TREMOLO 2010–current
CLASSIC VIBE TELECASTER CUSTOM 2010–current
CLASSIC VIBE TELECASTER THINLINE 2010–current
STANDARD TELECASTER SH WITH BIGSBY FSR 2010

2011
EHSAAN NOORANI STRATOCASTER 2011–current
J MASCIS JAZZMASTER 2011–current
JOE TROHMAN TELECASTER 2011–current
STRATOCASTER GUITAR & CONTROLLER 2011–current
TELE HH FSR 2011
VINTAGE MODIFIED JAGUAR HH 2011–current
VINTAGE MODIFIED JAZZMASTER 2011–current

INDEX

A page number in *italic type* indicates an illustration. A page number in the range 127–149 indicates an entry in the Reference Listing. Signature models are listed by the first word of the name, not the surname; for example, the Avril Lavigne model is found under A, not L.

ACKNOWLEDGEMENTS

INSTRUMENT PICTURES

OWNERS KEY
The guitars we've photographed came from the collections of the following individuals and organisations, and we are most grateful for their help. The owners are listed here in the alphabetical order of the code that is used to identify their instruments in the Instruments Key below. **AG** Arbiter Group; **BM** Barry Moorhouse; **DM** Dixie's Music; **FE** Fender Musical Instruments Corp; **GM** Geoff Malkin; **LT** Larry Thomas; **PD** Paul Day; **PR** Paul Rumble; **RC** Ray Craigie; **TB** Tony Bacon.

INSTRUMENTS KEY
This key identifies who owned which guitars at the time they were photographed. After the relevant **bold-type** page number(s) there is a model identifier followed by the owner's initials (see the alphabetical list in the Owners Key above). **22–23** Greco PR. **23** Fender Bullet DM. **26–27** Strat PR. **30–31** Tele GM. **31** Strat BM. **34–35** Strat PR. **35** Bullets both RC. **38–39** Strat TB. **42–43** Two guitars FE. **46** H.M. V FE. **46–47** H.M. II FE. **50–51** Silver Series both RC. **54** Bullet FE. **54–55** Strat LT. **58–59** Strat black FE, Strat blonde PR. **59** Tele FE. **62–63** Jagmaster FE. **63** Venus AG, Venus XII FE, Super-Sonic FE. **66–67** Four guitars FE. **70–71** Three guitars FE. **74–75** Two guitars FE. **78–79** Two guitars FE. **82–83** Three guitars FE. **86–87** Three guitars FE. **90** '51 blonde/black FE. **90–91** '51 blonde/white PD, '51 sunburst and '51 black both FE. **94** '51 blue FE. **94–95** '51 black and '51 sunburst both PD. **98–99** Two guitars FE. **102–103** Four guitars FE. **106–107** Two guitars FE. **110–111** Duo Sonic FE, Strat PR. **114–115** Two guitars both FE. **118–119** Three guitars FE.

Guitar photography for Backbeat UK was by Stephen Morris and Miki Slingsby.

ARTIST PICTURES
Images are identified by bold-type page number, subject, and photographer and/or collection and agency.

34 Murray, Ebet Roberts/Redferns/Getty Images. **47** Harrison, Lynn Hilton/Mail On Sunday/Rex Features. **55** Healey, Lorne Resnick/Redferns/Getty Images. **62** Rossdale, Mick Hutson/Redferns/Getty Images; Love, Mick Hutson/Redferns/Getty Images. **95** Curran, Alan Grossman. **99** Slash, Mark Sullivan/WireImage/Getty Images. **103** Fairey, Jon Furlong. **115** Prophet, Jordi Vidal/Redferns/Getty Images.

MEMORABILIA
Other items illustrated in this book – including advertisements, brochures, catalogues, and photographs (in fact anything that isn't a guitar or an artist shot) – came from the collections of Tony Bacon; Mary Steffek Blaske; Rainer Daeschler; Paul Day; Ken Feist; Fender Musical Instruments Corp; Bob Hipp; *Japan Music Trades*; Peter Pulham; Dan Smith; Vintaxe.com.

INTERVIEWS
Original interviews used in this book were conducted by Tony Bacon as follows: **Roger Balmer** (May 2011); **Keith Brawley** (June 2011); **Billy Bush** (July 2011); **Joe Carducci** (November 1997, May 2011); **Shepard Fairey** (July 2011); **John 5** (May 2011); **Martin Fredman** (May 2011); **Chris Gill** (April 2011); **Mike Lewis** (May 2011); **Clay Lyons** (May 2011); **Graeme Mathieson** (May 2011); **Richard McDonald** (May 2011); **Bill Mendello** (June 2011); **Ehsaan Noorani** (May 2011); **Justin**

Norvell (April 2011); **John Page** (May 2011); **Alex Perez** (May 2011); **Steve Preston** (May 2011); **Billy Siegle** (May 2011); **Dan Smith** (February 1985, February 1992, June 2005, May 2011); **Nick Sugimoto** (May 2011); **Mike Tonn** (May 2011); **Brad Townsend** (May 2011); **Andy Zuckerman** (May 2011).

THANKS

In addition to those already named in Instrument Pictures, Artist Pictures, Memorabilia, and Original Interviews, the author would like to thank: Julie Bowie, Joe Allrich, Tony Arambarri (NAMM); Brandy Barker (Fender); George Blanda (Fender); Steve Brown (vintaxe.com); John Callaghan (*Guitar & Bass*); Larry Cashdollar (21frets.com); Gary Cooper (*Guitar Interactive*); Paul Cooper; Paul Cross; Dan Del Fiorentino (NAMM); Naoko Doi; André Duchossoir; Terry Foster; John Hill; Martin Kelly; Mark Keraly (Fender); Masako Koyama (*Japan Music Trades*); Brian Majeski (*The Music Trades*); Neville Marten (*Guitar Techniques*); Peter McGovern; John Morrish; Andrew Munro; Ace Nakata; Heinz Rebellius; Paul Rivera (Rivera Amplification); Takahiro 'Johnny' Saitoh; Sam Sekihara (Dyna Boeki); Tina Soikkeli (Obey Giant); Billy Squier; Steve Squier; Sami Stenholm; Kazuma Tanabe (FGN Guitars); Mark Thomas (*Guitarist*); Chip Todd; Harry Turner (H.L. Turner Co).

SPECIAL THANKS

Paul Day for researching and writing the reference section and helpful counsel; **Jason Farrell** (Fender) for contacts and help and intelligence and everything else in between; **Ken Feist** (ex-Fender) for digging out and sending a pile of valuable memorabilia; **Bob Hipp** (ex-Fender) for the loan of three big binders of fine memorabilia; **Paul Rumble** for hands-on collecting experience and considered advice; **Dan Smith** (ex-Fender) for being there and remembering; and **Bob Willocks** (Fender) for sharing the details.

BOOKS

Tony Bacon *The Fender Electric Guitar Book: A Complete History Of Fender Instruments* (Backbeat 2007); *Six Decades Of The Fender Telecaster: The Story Of The World's First Solidbody Electric Guitar* (Backbeat 2005); *60 Years Of Fender: Six Decades Of The Greatest Electric Guitars* (Backbeat 2010); *The Stratocaster Guitar Book: A Complete History Of Fender Stratocaster Guitars* (Backbeat 2010).
Tony Bacon (ed) *Electric Guitars: The Illustrated Encyclopedia* (Thunder Bay 2000).
Paul Specht with Michael Wright & Jim Donahue *Ibanez: The Untold Story* (Hoshino 2005).
Victor Carroll Squier *Antonio Stradivari: His Life And Work 1644–1737* (Kessinger, undated reprint of original 1944 edition).

MAGAZINES

We consulted various back issues of the following magazines and newspapers: *Billboard*; *Electronics & Music Maker*; *Fender Frontline*; *Guitar Player*; *Japan Music Trades*; *Melody Maker*; *The Music Trades*; *Music World*; *Musician*; *Up Beat*.

WEBSITES

The site we visited most often during research was, inevitably, the official one: www.squierguitars.com. As we went to press, this was incorporated into the main Fender site at www.fender.com. Another good source of info, especially on the early Squier guitars, is the JV Chronicles at www.21frets.com/squier_jv/index.htm. Forums and message boards can offer nuggets of good info among the unsubstantiated speculation. Those we found best were: the JV Forum (not in fact limited to the JV period) at www.21frets.com /cgi-bin/forum/Blah.pl?; Squier-Talk at www.squier-talk.com/forum/index.php; and the Squier Strat Forum at strat-talk.com.

TRADEMARKS

Throughout this book we have mentioned a number of registered trademark names. Rather than put a trademark or registered symbol next to every occurrence of a trademarked name, we state here that we are using the names only in an editorial fashion and that we do not intend to infringe any trademarks.

UPDATES?

The author and publisher welcome any new information for future editions. Write to: Squier Electrics, Backbeat & Jawbone, 2A Union Court, 20-22 Union Road, London SW4 6JP, England. Or you can email: squier@jawbonepress.com.

"Squier is a brand that we can mess with a little bit – and that doesn't upset the consumer. In fact, they kind of expect that from the brand. Whereas with Fender, if you move a screw a millimetre to the left, you get hate mail." *Clay Lyons, Fender Musical Instruments Corp*